Excel
Basic Skills

T0342989

Year 6
Ages 11-12

English and Mathematics

Get the Results You Want!

PASCAL
PRESS

Contents

Introduction

The **Excel** Basic Skills Workbook series aims to build and reinforce basic skills in reading, comprehension and mathematics.

The series has eight English and Mathematics core books, one for each of the school years Kindergarten/Foundation to Year 7. These are supported by teaching books, which can be used if the student needs help in a particular area of study.

The structure of this book

This book has 30 carefully sequenced double-page units. Each unit has work on Number and Algebra, Measurement and Geometry, and Statistics and Probability in Maths, and Reading and Comprehension, Spelling and Vocabulary, and Grammar and Punctuation in English.

The student's competence in each of the 30 units can be recorded on the marking grid on pages 5 and 7. There are four end-of-term reviews. These are referred to as Tests 1 to 4. They assess the student's understanding of work covered during each term.

How to use this book

It is recommended that students complete each unit in the sequence provided because the knowledge and understanding developed in each unit is consolidated and practised in subsequent units. The workbook can be used to cover core classroom work. It can also be used to provide homework and consolidation activities.

All units are written so that particular questions deal with the same areas of learning in each unit. For example, question 1 is always on Number (addition) and question 11 is always on Measurement (time), and so on. Similarly in the English units question 1 is always on Reading and Comprehension, and question 14 is always on Punctuation. Question formatting is repeated throughout the workbook to support familiarity so that students can more readily deal with the Mathematics and English content.

The marking grids (see the examples on pages 4 and 6) are easy-to-use tools for recording students' progress. If you find that certain questions are repeatedly causing difficulties and errors, then there is a specific **Excel** Basic/Advanced Skills Workbook to help students fully revise that topic.

These are the teaching books of the series; they will take students through the topic step by step. The use of illustrations and diagrams, practice questions, and a straightforward and simple approach will make some of the most common problem areas of English and Mathematics easy to understand and master.

Sample Maths Marking Grid

If a student is consistently getting more than **one in five** questions wrong in any area, refer to the highlighted *Excel* Basic/Advanced Skills title. When marking answers on the grid, simply mark incorrect answers with 'X' in the appropriate box. This will result in a graphical representation of areas needing further work. An example has been done below for the first seven units. If a question has several parts, it should be counted as wrong if one or more mistakes are made.

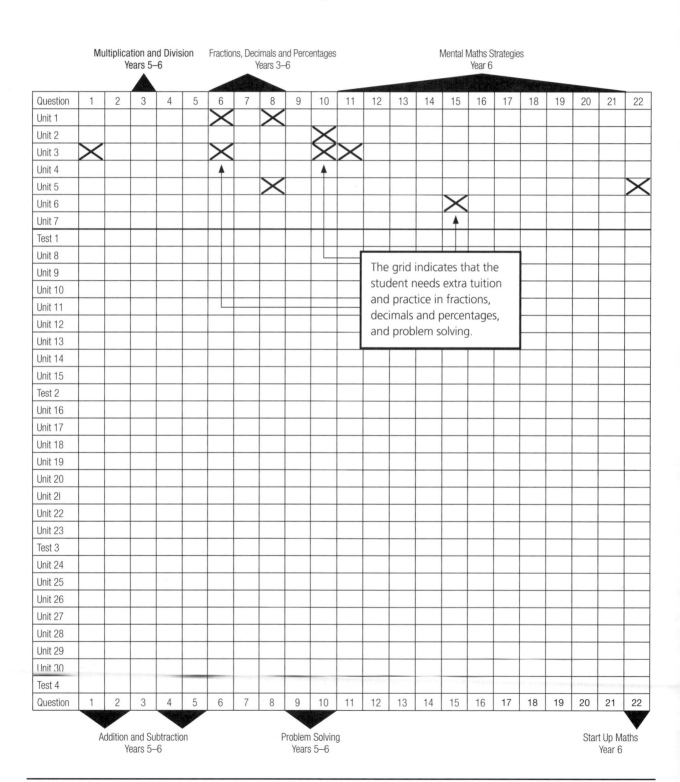

Multiplication and Division Years 5–6

Fractions, Decimals and Percentages Years 3–6

Mental Maths Strategies Year 6

The grid indicates that the student needs extra tuition and practice in fractions, decimals and percentages, and problem solving.

Addition and Subtraction Years 5–6

Problem Solving Years 5–6

Start Up Maths Year 6

Maths Marking Grid

Question	Addition	Subtraction	Division/Multiplication	Place Value	Number Patterns	Fractions	Money	Decimals/Percentages	Estimating	Problem Solving	Time	Mass	Length/Perimeter	Area	Volume/Capacity	Temperature	2D & 3D Shapes	Angles	Symmetry/Transformation	Direction/Coordinates	Graphs	Statistics and Probability
Question	1	2	3	4	5	6	7	8	9	10	11	12	13	14	15	16	17	18	19	20	21	22
Unit 1																						
Unit 2																						
Unit 3																						
Unit 4																						
Unit 5																						
Unit 6																						
Unit 7																						
Test 1																						
Unit 8																						
Unit 9																						
Unit 10																						
Unit 11																						
Unit 12																						
Unit 13																						
Unit 14																						
Unit 15																						
Test 2																						
Unit 16																						
Unit 17																						
Unit 18																						
Unit 19																						
Unit 20																						
Unit 21																						
Unit 22																						
Unit 23																						
Test 3																						
Unit 24																						
Unit 25																						
Unit 26																						
Unit 27																						
Unit 28																						
Unit 29																						
Unit 30																						
Test 4																						
Question	1	2	3	4	5	6	7	8	9	10	11	12	13	14	15	16	17	18	19	20	21	22

Sample English Marking Grid

If a student is consistently getting more than **one in five** questions wrong in any area, refer to the highlighted **_Excel_** Basic Skills title. When marking answers on the grid, simply mark incorrect answers with 'X' in the appropriate box. This will result in a graphical representation of areas needing further work. An example has been done below for the first seven units.

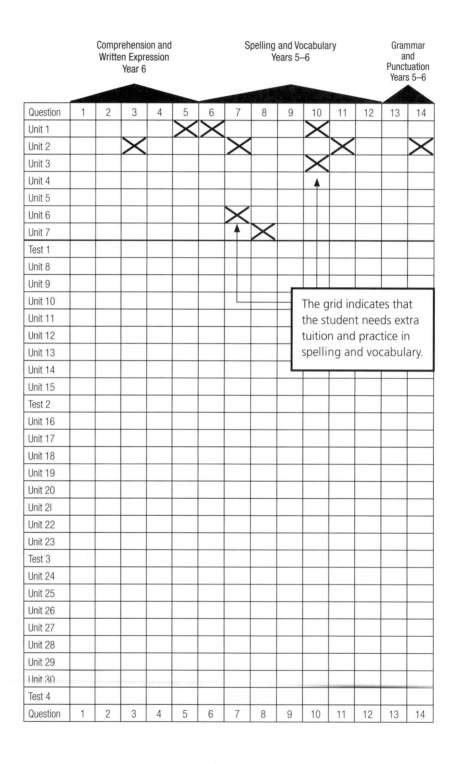

The grid indicates that the student needs extra tuition and practice in spelling and vocabulary.

English Marking Grid

Question	Reading and Comprehension					Spelling and Vocabulary							Grammar and Punctuation	
	1	2	3	4	5	6	7	8	9	10	11	12	13	14
Unit 1														
Unit 2														
Unit 3														
Unit 4														
Unit 5														
Unit 6														
Unit 7														
Test 1														
Unit 8														
Unit 9														
Unit 10														
Unit 11														
Unit 12														
Unit 13														
Unit 14														
Unit 15														
Test 2														
Unit 16														
Unit 17														
Unit 18														
Unit 19														
Unit 20														
Unit 21														
Unit 22														
Unit 23														
Test 3														
Unit 24														
Unit 25														
Unit 26														
Unit 27														
Unit 28														
Unit 29														
Unit 30														
Test 4														
Question	1	2	3	4	5	6	7	8	9	10	11	12	13	14

Number and Algebra

1.

+	7	8	6	2	9	16
5						

2.

−	8	7	15	9	12	32
6						

3.

×	9	2	4	6	7	12
8						

4. Write thirty-seven thousand eight hundred and sixty-one in digits.

5. 163, 165, 167, [   ] , [   ] , [   ]

6. Write one and four tenths in decimal form.

7. What change will I get from a $50 note?

8. Show 3.47 on this abacus.

9. Round off 186 574 to the nearest 10 000.

10. What is the minimum number of notes and coins needed to give $34.85 change?

Measurement and Geometry

11. Write ten to eight at night in am/pm time.

12. My dog won't stand on the scales. How can I find its mass?

13. Write in mm: 2 cm 4 mm.

14. Calculate the area.

6 m
4 m

15. 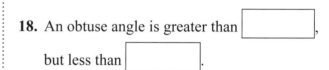 How many centicubes were used to build this model?

16. Write forty-five degrees Celsius in shortened form.

17. Here are the views of a shape. Name it.
Front   Top

18. An obtuse angle is greater than [   ] , but less than [   ] .

19. Draw in the lines of symmetry.

20. 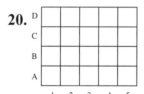 Place a cross in the square (3, B) and shade in (2, D).

Statistics and Probability

21. This line has been drawn to the scale of 1 : 10. How long was the real line?

22. What are the possible outcomes when a die is rolled?

A secret message

Two soldiers armed with two flashing scimitars barged past the front gate of the small house. They marched through the beautifully kept rose garden and knocked loudly on the front door. A white bearded old man appeared, holding a page in one hand, and a quill in the other. The page was filled with a triangular pattern of numbers.

"We want Omar Khayyam", one soldier yelled at him.

"I'm Omar Khayyam", the old man replied softly.

"The vizier wants you!"

The year was AD 1113, the place Naishapur in Persia.

A look of fear crossed Omar's face. Since the new vizier had come to power, many people had been arrested. Some had been executed.

Omar wondered why he had been summoned, but he reassured himself he had nothing to worry about—he had not committed a crime, and the poems he wrote were personal and only his friends had read them.

From *Additional Fables* by Rolf Grunseit

Reading and Comprehension

1. Who yelled at Omar?
   (a) the vizier   (b) a soldier
   (c) an old man   (d) Khayyam

2. Omar wondered why he had been summoned. Was it for
   (a) a crime he had committed?
   (b) execution?
   (c) his friends' wishes?
   (d) something he knew nothing about?

3. Omar was holding a quill in his hand. The quill was used
   (a) to write with.
   (b) to point at the numbers.
   (c) to poke holes in the paper to record numbers.
   (d) to tend his beard.

4. In which country does this story take place?

   _____

5. Number these sentences in order (1–4).
   (a) Omar had been working on Mathematics.
   (b) The vizier ordered his soldiers to collect Omar.
   (c) Omar was very surprised.
   (d) The soldiers marched through the garden.

Spelling and Vocabulary

Rewrite the misspelt words.

6. The bandige is too tight. _____

7. This anser is corect. _____

Circle the word that has the nearest meaning to the underlined word.

8. What a <u>sleek</u> car.
   (a) valuable   (b) smooth
   (c) red   (d) old

9. Do you <u>possess</u> a gun?
   (a) shoot   (b) own
   (c) carry   (d) fire

Circle the correct word in brackets.

10. Sam and George (was, were) at the circus.

11. All of you (has, have) the wrong answer.

12. A purse holding three dollars (was, were) found.

Grammar and Punctuation

13. Which are the nouns in this sentence?

    Bass and Flinders sailed from Sydney in the *Tom Thumb*.

    _____

    _____

14. Punctuate and capitalise this sentence.

    he muttered it isnt fair

    _____

    _____

Number and Algebra

1.

+	8	5	9	6	7	19
2						

2.

–	18	10	16	12	14	37
9						

3.

÷	15	5	20	10	30	45
5						

4. Write 47 198 in words.

5. 2042, 2044, 2046,

⬚ , ⬚ , ⬚

6. Shade $\dfrac{5}{6}$ on this model.

7. What is the least number of notes and coins I can be given as change from a \$50 note after spending \$16.45?

8. What number is shown on this abacus?

9. 56 847 rounded off to the nearest 100 is:

10. What number taken from 19.3 will give 8.62?

Measurement and Geometry

11. It's now 11:35 am. What will the time be in $\dfrac{1}{2}$ hour?

12. An empty jar has a mass of 78 g. When it is full of jam it has a mass of 353 g. What mass of jam is in the jar?

13. What is the exact length of this line segment, in mm?

14. What is the area of this square? 1.5 m

15. 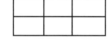 3 cm 4 cm 5 cm
How many centicubes could fill this space?

16. Minus seventeen degrees Celsius can be written as:

17. Draw the net of an open cube.

18. What type of angle is 37°?

19. A B C D E F G H

Mark in the lines of symmetry on each letter.

20. To find the co-ordinates you go:
(a) vertically then horizontally
(b) horizontally then vertically

Statistics and Probability

21. This boy is drawn to scale (1 : 100). What is his height?

22. For every 20 books that I read I was given a sticker. How many stickers did I receive?

Beowulf's downfall

King Beowulf Waymunding had seen thirty winters before he became king of the Gauts. He kept the kingdom well for fifty more, until the hoard-guarding dragon, Hringboga, awoke, and in the dark nights began to rule.

For three hundred winters this destroyer of nations had slept beneath an ancient burial mound. That mound was built upon Earnaness; a headland by the sea. Dragons, it seems, have always sought for hidden treasures. So it was, that Hringboga found in that place a wealth of undefended joy.

No-one but Hringboga knew the way into the burial mound. Yet one man did enter. There, his hand fell upon a golden cup, and so aroused Hringboga's anger. The man who caused the dragon's pain had not intended it. He was only a lowly slave, on the run from a flogging. Needing shelter, he had felt his way into the burial mound. When he saw Hringboga sleeping there, fear turned his guts to water. Yet upon seeing the heaps of gold that were the dragon's bed, his fear gave way to an idea …

Thinking to make a peace-offering to his master, the slave grabbed a precious cup and took it with him. He believed the dragon would never miss a thing so small. He was wrong.

From *Beowulf's Downfall* by Brad Turner

Reading and Comprehension

1. The dragon's lair was in
   (a) Waumunding.
   (b) Earnaness.
   (c) Hringboga.
   (d) the burial mound.

2. For how many years had the dragon slept?
   (a) thirty winters   (b) fifty winters
   (c) 300 years   (d) all winter

3. Hringboga was angry because
   (a) a slave entered the lair.
   (b) a gold cup was taken.
   (c) gold had been stolen.
   (d) it was winter.

4. Why did the slave steal the golden cup?

   _____

   _____

5. Number these sentences in order (1–4).
   (a) He stole the cup as a peace-offering for his master.
   (b) Dragons always seek out hidden treasures.
   (c) A lowly slave entered the dragon's lair.
   (d) When he saw the dragon the slave was afraid.

Spelling and Vocabulary

Rewrite the misspelt words.

6. Quiet or you'll startel the animals.

   _____

7. I like mistery stories. _____

Circle the word that has the nearest meaning to the underlined word.

8. The sounds were <u>simultaneous</u>.
   (a) loud   (b) soft
   (c) together   (d) deafening

9. He gave me a <u>haughty</u> look.
   (a) sad   (b) happy   (c) nasty   (d) proud

Circle the correct word in brackets.

10. The stars (is, are) bright tonight.

11. His friend and (he, him) travelled to Cairns.

12. Fred is younger than (I, me).

Grammar and Punctuation

13. Use *herd* in a sentence as a verb.

   _____

   _____

14. Punctuate and capitalise this sentence.

   where are you going asked jim

   _____

   _____

Mathematics

Number and Algebra

1.

+	0	7	3	5	9	17
8						

2.

−	7	11	5	9	3	39
3						

3.

×	2	7	3	8	6	12
3						

4. What is the value of 6 in 146 027?

5. 2, 3, 5, 8, ___ , ___ , ___

6. What fraction is shaded?

7. From a balance of $186.45 Tina withdrew $29.50. The balance now is:

8. What is the value of the 2 in 3.25?

9. 756 cm rounded to the nearest metre is:

10. Eight people shared a Lotto prize of $9000. How much did each receive?

Measurement and Geometry

11. Write 1:03 pm in 24-hour time.

12. Egg cartons have a mass of 35 g. What is the gross mass of a carton of a dozen 60-gram eggs?

13. Write 105 mm in cm.

14. 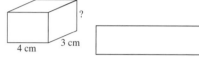 This rectangular paddock has an area of ___ square metres.

15. 60 centicubes fill this shape. Find the missing dimensions.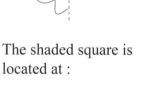

16. What is the difference between 14 °C and −5 °C?

17. This is the net of an open rectangular prism. True or false?

18. Measure this angle.

19. Finish the shape to make it symmetrical.

20. 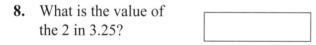 The shaded square is located at :

Statistics and Probability

21. A building is 38 metres tall. If it is drawn to scale, 1 : 1000, how tall will the drawing be?

22. This tally shows the points scored in a game.

Jen 卌 卌 卌 卌 卌 ||
David 卌 卌 卌 卌 卌 ||||
Matthew 卌 卌 卌 |||

How many points were scored altogether?

Dear diary.

I haven't told you about Tracy have I? Tracy is the continuity person. She has a really hard job. I know there's NO WAY I could do it. She has to watch every scene to make sure that everything matches up with the last one. Say that I had my school jumper on yesterday, and today I didn't have it on. We are doing the same scene as yesterday. If Tracy doesn't say "Put your jumper on", then when they edit the film in the studio afterwards, I'll have my jumper on and off, on and off, and it will look really strange.

Funny actually! There are a thousand little things which Tracy has to keep an eye out for. If there's a mistake then someone will see it and we will be on 'Hey Hey It's Saturday'.

Ah, we are here—the dreaded make-up van.

From *My Diary* by Jenny Jarman-Walker

Reading and Comprehension

1. Penny, the author of this diary entry
   (a) wants to be a continuity person.
   (b) is leaving to be a continuity person.
   (c) thinks she doesn't have the skills.
   (d) likes a hard job.

2. Tracy's job is to try and prevent
   (a) actors making mistakes.
   (b) little details being missed.
   (c) actors forgetting to wear jumpers.
   (d) make-up being wasted.

3. The continuity person checks the details
   (a) before shooting the scene.
   (b) after the scene is shot.
   (c) during editing.
   (d) during the scenes.

4. Name the TV show which often has 'bloopers'.

_____

5. Number these sentences in order (1–4).
   (a) She will need make-up first before shooting the scene.
   (b) Penny is an actress.
   (c) She is playing the part of a school girl.
   (d) She is working on the same scene as yesterday.

Spelling and Vocabulary

Rewrite the misspelt words.

6. He's a briliant student.

_____

7. I watched the prosession.

_____

Circle the word that has the nearest meaning to the underlined word.

8. We waited <u>anxiously</u> for Pete to return.
   (a) quietly   (b) fearfully
   (c) silently   (d) a long time

9. His <u>mastery</u> of the game was obvious.
   (a) lack of knowledge   (b) great knowledge
   (c) understanding   (d) playing

Circle the correct word in brackets.

10. Sonja has (grew, grown) tall.

11. The crier (rang, rung) the bell.

12. Has he (wrote, written) to his uncle?

Grammar and Punctuation

13. Rewrite this sentence so that it talks about the past.

   I do my work on time.

_____

14. Punctuate and capitalise this sentence.

   youll find that theres more gold here than weve ever seen

_____

_____

Number and Algebra

1.

+	3	2	5	8	6	11
9						

2.
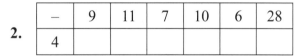

–	9	11	7	10	6	28
4						

3.

÷	56	28	49	14	21	42
7						

4. Show 268 193 on this abacus.

H.Th T.Th Th H T U

5. 4, 6, 8, 9, 10, ☐ , ☐ , ☐

6. Write twelve and fourteen hundredths in decimal form. ☐

7. After spending from a $50 note I have $32.75 change. I have spent: ☐

8. Write the number made up of 2 units, 7 tenths and 4 hundredths. ☐

9. To the nearest litre, round off 1642 mL. ☐

10. How many minutes are there in July? ☐

Measurement and Geometry

11.

= ☐ am = ☐
24-hour time

12. An unloaded truck has a mass of 8.95 t. Fully loaded it has a mass of 17.02 t. What is the mass of its load? ☐

13. Put in the correct unit.
Jill is 1.53 ☐ tall.

14. The length of a rectangle is 47 cm. The width is 38 mm. Before I can calculate the area I must:
☐

15. Which has the greater volume?
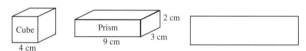
Cube 4 cm
Prism 9 cm 3 cm 2 cm
☐

16. It's now 18 ˚C. If the temperature falls 25˚, the temperature will be: ☐

17. How many vertices has a triangular-based pyramid? ☐

18. An angle greater than 180˚, but less than 360˚ is a ☐ angle.

19. Draw in the lines of symmetry in this octagon.

20. If → is north, then ↓ indicates: ☐

21. Under a 75× microscope, a flea appears to be 75 mm long. In real life how long is the flea? ☐

Statistics and Probability

22. This tally shows the number of different trees in a park. If 6 Wattles, 4 Tea trees and 17 Gum trees were removed, how many would be left? ☐

Type of tree	Wattle	Tea tree	Gum	Elm
Number	|||| |||| |||| |||	|||| |||| ||	|||| |||| |||| |||| |||| ||||	|||

Strange mysteries

One interesting story regarding some wreckage found in the Bermuda Triangle concerns a small German Second World War aircraft, the *Arado*, which was found by divers near Bermuda in 1963. Although it had been in the water for about twenty years, the plane had been perfectly preserved!

It had no bullet holes, no burns, no missing parts. It was not even rusty. Even the wiring and hydraulic lines were completely intact. The engine was 'clean as a whistle'. A chemical analysis of its paint suggested that it could not have been under sea water for twenty years, but there it was, with no bodies, no skeletons, not a single thing inside. Just a clean, empty plane.

There was absolutely no clue as to why it had crashed and sunk. The Bermuda Triangle, which you can find on your atlas, is in the Atlantic Ocean, bound by an imaginary line connecting Florida, Bermuda and Puerto Rico. *From Strange Mysteries by Rachael Collinson*

Reading and Comprehension

1. The Bermuda Triangle is to be found in
   (a) the Atlantic Ocean. (b) Florida.
   (c) Bermuda. (c) Puerto Rico.

2. Inside the plane divers found
   (a) bodies. (b) skeletons.
   (c) nothing. (d) everything intact.

3. The cause of the crash was
   (a) bullets. (b) fire.
   (c) engine failure. (d) not explained.

4. Even though it had disappeared twenty years before, it had not rusted.

   True or false? _____

5. Number these sentences in order (1–4).
   (a) It was perfectly preserved.
   (b) The *Arado* disappeared during WW2.
   (c) It could not have been under water for twenty years.
   (d) Some divers found it twenty years later.

Spelling and Vocabulary

Rewrite the misspelt words.

6. What's the purpos of this? _____

7. They won the competitition.

   _____

Circle the word that has the nearest meaning to the underlined word.

8. He waited till the noise subsided.
   (a) increased   (b) decreased
   (c) stopped   (d) started

9. She was rewarded for her persistence.
   (a) work   (b) good looks
   (c) patience   (d) continued effort

Circle the correct word in brackets.

10. The leopard (sprung, sprang) at its prey.

11. He neither reads (or, nor) writes well.

12. Charles is stronger (as, than) me.

Grammar and Punctuation

13. Combine these sentences into one sentence.

    A crow was thirsty. He flew to the tank. He hoped that there would be water in it.

    _____

    _____

    _____

14. Punctuate and capitalise this sentence.

    its a flock of emus stated ken

    _____

    _____

Number and Algebra

1.

+	1	7	5	6	0	18
4						

2.

−	9	16	11	13	14	26
8						

3.

×	5	0	1	6	9	10
6						

4. 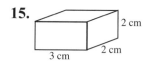 What number is shown on this abacus?

5. 695, 690, 685, ___ , ___ , ___

6. Write the fraction for sixteen out of twenty.

7. Had $3.95. Found 45 cents. Spent $1.60. Now I have:

8. 7.35 is made out of ___ units, ___ tenths, and ___ hundredths.

9. 456 minutes rounds off to ___ hours.

10. My odometer read 17 586.2 when I left home and 19 638.8 when I got back. How far did I travel before I turned back?

Measurement and Geometry

11. Show a quarter to twelve in the morning on these clocks.

12. What unit of mass is used to measure a truck?

13. Measure the length and breadth of this rectangle, and then calculate the perimeter.

14. To have an area of 1 square metre, I must have a square shape with a side of one metre. True or false?

15.  This shape has a volume of 12 cm³. If I double all dimensions, the volume is now:

16. Is normal body temperature 0 °C, 37 °C or 100 °C?

17. How many edges are to be found on a rectangular prism?

18. Measure this angle.

19. How many lines of symmetry are to be found in a circle?

20. What direction is 45° clockwise from due east?

21. Draw a rectangle 3 m long × $1\frac{1}{2}$ m wide to the scale of 1 : 100.

Statistics and Probability

22. ▢ = 10 books

Class	No. of books				
6R	▢	▢	▢		
6J	▢	▢	▢	▢	⌐
6F	▢	▢			
6M	▢	▢	▢	⌐	

4 classes entered a Read-a-thon. How many books were read altogether?

How can we make a magnet?

The atoms in a bar of iron or steel can be made to line up in the same way by stroking the bar in one direction with a magnet. This turns the bar into a magnet. Because the atoms in iron and steel are easy to line up this way these two metals are used for making magnets.

Magnets can be made another way. If a coil of wire carrying an electric current is wound around an iron bar, the atoms in the electric wire force the atoms in the bar to line up and face the same way. The bar then becomes a magnet. This type of magnet is called an electromagnet. Large electromagnets are used by cranes in the scrap metal industry. They can lift heavy metal objects like car bodies. When the electricity is switched on, the end of the crane becomes magnetic and it can pick up scrap iron. When the electricity is switched off it loses its magnetic effect and the iron is released. Much smaller electromagnets are found in such things as telephones, television tubes and computer screens. They are also used in electric motors and generators.

From *Tell Me How* by Mike Callaghan et al.

Reading and Comprehension

1. To make a nail into a magnet using a magnet
(a) stroke backwards and forward.
(b) stroke only forward.
(c) stroke only backwards.
(d) stroke in one direction only.

2. Electromagnets work
(a) when electrical current passes through the wire coil.
(b) when they are near other magnets.
(c) when you need them.
(d) only on cranes.

3. Small electromagnets are not to be found in
(a) computer screens.
(b) telephones.
(c) ship's compasses.
(d) electric motors.

4. Magnets are made of _____ or
_____ .

5. Number these sentences in order (1–4).
(a) Pass an electric current through the wire.
(b) Take an iron bar.
(c) Turn the current off when you no longer need the magnet.
(d) Coil wire around the bar.

Spelling and Vocabulary

Rewrite the misspelt words.

6. He's my bother. _____

7. The current is quite tasty. _____

Circle the word that has the nearest meaning to the underlined word.

8. The <u>exposed</u> film is in the container.
(a) new   (b) used
(c) old   (d) valuable

9. He was able to <u>acquire</u> more land.
(a) get   (b) sell   (c) see   (d) use

Circle the correct word in brackets.

10. The ship berthed at the (key, quay).

11. She is not (aloud, allowed) to go.

12. This material is (coarse, course).

Grammar and Punctuation

13. Write the plurals of the following words.

wife   _____

gas   _____

sheep   _____

14. Punctuate and capitalise this sentence.

youll have to travel along jones road till you come to wilsons crossing

_____

_____

_____

Number and Algebra

1.

+	7	5	0	6	9	29
1						

2.

–	10	8	6	14	12	45
5						

3.

÷	10	18	6	14	2	48
2						

4. Expand 168 574.

+	+	+	+	+

5. 1495, 1395, 1295, [____] , [____] , [____]

6. Write the fraction with a denominator of 8 and a numerator of 3.

7. On a balance of $874.60, $13.95 interest was paid. The balance now is:

8. In 7.69, which digit has the greatest value?

9. Circle the numbers which round to 5000.
4198   4981   4819   4918

10. A book has 128 pages. There are an average of 31 lines per page. On each line is an average of 16 five-letter words. How many letters are in the book?

Measurement and Geometry

11. 13:46 = [____] am / pm

12. Which is heavier, a tonne of feathers or 1000 kg of gold?

13. A square with a side of 16 cm has a perimeter of [____] cm?

14. Area is:
(a) the measurement of the distance around the edge of the shape, or
(b) the measurement of the space contained within the shape.

15. A rectangular prism with dimensions of 6 cm, 30 mm and 40 mm, has a cubic capacity of [____] cm³.

16. 34 °C outside in the sun and –12 °C in the freezer. What is the difference in temperature?

17. Name the shape in which all views are a circle.

18. What is the size of the angle marked (a)?

19. If BC is the line of symmetry, what was the original shape?

20. I'm travelling north-west. If I turn 90° anticlockwise, I'll be travelling [____].

21.  The scale in this photograph is 1 : 800. How tall is the tree?

Statistics and Probability

22. Colour in this spinner so that blue and green have a similar chance, but red has the best chance of all.

What is global warming?

The word 'global' refers to the land, sea and atmosphere of the planet earth. Global warming is the result of the sun's radiation being absorbed by gases in the atmosphere. These gases are known as greenhouse gases. Changes in the temperature of the atmosphere affect the movement of the air around the globe. This, in turn, causes the weather patterns around the world to change. If the global warming is too great, it will severely change the world's weather systems which will in turn have a disastrous effect on life on earth.

Scientific evidence shows that there are many more greenhouse gases today than ever before. This number is growing, mainly because of the energy we use in factories and at home. That is why many scientists say that the greenhouse effect must not be ignored and why we must all try to help reduce greenhouse gases to avoid the risk of global warming.

Small changes to the average temperature on earth can cause major changes to the earth's climate. Evidence shows that during the last Ice Age the temperature was only an average of four degrees colder than today. This was enough, however, to cause the ice from the polar regions to spread and cover an enormous area of the earth's surface.

From *Technology for the Environment*
by Mike Callaghan & Peter Knapp

Reading and Comprehension

1. Global warming is caused by
   (a) the sun's radiation.
   (b) greenhouse gases.
   (c) our atmosphere.
   (d) the sun's radiation being absorbed by greenhouse gases.

2. To reduce global warming we must
   (a) reduce the sun's energy.
   (b) reduce greenhouse gases.
   (c) change weather patterns.
   (d) listen to scientists.

3. Temperature has a great effect on
   (a) weather.   (b) the earth.
   (c) greenhouse gases. (d) global warming.

4. During the Ice Age the temperature dropped

   by _____°.

5. Number these sentences in order (1–4).
   (a) Our atmosphere becomes warmer.
   (b) We produce more greenhouse gases than ever before.
   (c) Warmer conditions affect our climate.
   (d) Greenhouse gases absorb energy from the sun.

Spelling and Vocabulary

Rewrite the misspelt words.

6. Too emus were seen on the plain.

   _____

7. The enemy stormed the fought.

   _____

Circle the word that has the nearest meaning to the underlined word.

8. This is a <u>radical</u> change.
   (a) good   (b) complete   (c) bad   (d) rapid

9. I will <u>negotiate</u> the new deal.
   (a) arrange   (b) complete
   (c) fix   (d) talk about

Circle the correct word in brackets.

10. The moon is (pail, pale) tonight.

11. We walked along the (beech, beach).

12. His pencil was (broke, broken).

Grammar and Punctuation

13. Insert the missing word.

    Our house is different _____ yours.

14. Punctuate and capitalise this sentence.

    the pup said the farmers wife is hungry

    _____

    _____

Number and Algebra

1.

+	2	7	4	0	8	24
6						

2.

–	14	15	12	10	13	47
7						

3.

×	4	6	2	3	8	10
5						

4. 200 000 + 60 000 + 5000 + 900 + 70 + 6 =

5. 5164, 6164, 7164, ____, ____, ____

6. Show $\frac{16}{16}$.

7. Balance $2872.45.
Withdrew $95.70.
New balance is:

8. In 3.68, which digit has the least value?

9. Give an approximate answer (in thousands) for

$$\begin{array}{r} 7564 \\ +\ 1893 \\ \hline \end{array}$$

10. Find the product when the sum of 59 and 46 is multiplied by their difference.

Measurement and Geometry

11. Is 7:15 pm the same as 1915 hours or 0715 hours?

12. A packet of pasta is labelled 500 g. I put it on the scales. The scales read 513 g. Explain why.

13. A rectangle is 10 mm wide and 10 cm long. What is its perimeter in cm?

14. Calculate the area of a rectangle 10 mm wide and 10 cm long.

15. A tin in the shape of a rectangular prism, L = 5 cm, W = 4 cm, H = 10 cm, will hold [   ] cm³ of water.

16. What is the temperature on this thermometer?

20°   40°   60°

17. The following is the net of a rectangular prism. True or false?

18. Name the instrument used to measure angles.

19. Draw in the lines of symmetry in this shape.

20. Name (using initials) the points on this compass.

21. The distance between town A and town B on the map is 3.2 cm. If the scale is 1 : 100 000, then they are [   ] km apart.

Statistics and Probability

22.

 = 5 votes

Children voted for their favourite sport. How many children voted?

Sport	No. of votes
Football	⚥ ⚥ ⚥ ⚥ ⚥
Tennis	⚥ ⚥ ⚥
Soccer	⚥ ⚥ ⚥ ⚥ ⚥ ⚥ ⚥
Netball	⚥ ⚥ ⚥ ⚥ ⚥ ⚥

Train from Melbourne to Sydney Departure Times

Melbourne	6:30 am
Benalla	8:22 am
Wangaratta	8:45 am
Albury	9:25 am
Wagga Wagga	10:43 am
Cootamundra	11:51 am
Harden	2:26 pm
Yass Junction	2:34 pm
Goulburn	3:25 pm
Moss Vale	4:15 pm
Sydney	5:15 pm

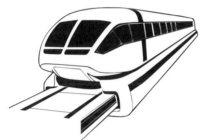

Reading and Comprehension

1. How long does it take to travel from Melbourne to
   (a) Albury? _____
   (b) Goulburn? _____

2. If you arrive at Wagga Wagga station at 9:30 am, how long must you wait before the train departs for Sydney?

   _____

3. Between which two towns is the travel time about six hours?

   _____

4. Which station is nearest to halfway in time to Sydney?

   _____

5. How long is the trip from Melbourne to Sydney?

   _____

Spelling and Vocabulary

Rewrite the misspelt words.

6. Heres what you want. _____

7. Let's practice what you've learned.

   _____

Circle the word that has the nearest meaning to the underlined word.

8. I presume you know the answer.
   (a) know
   (b) think
   (c) am
   (d) take for granted

9. Don't aggravate the animals.
   (a) annoy
   (b) feed
   (c) pat
   (d) startle

Circle the correct word in brackets.

10. They (tracked, tract) the animal to the cave.

11. She went (straight, strait) across the road.

12. The animal (paste, paced) up and down in the cage.

Grammar and Punctuation

13. Turn this sentence round.

    The dogs hunted the deer.

    _____

14. Punctuate and capitalise this sentence.

    mr a l jones helped ms t a smith with her speech

    _____

    _____

Mathematics

Number and Algebra

1. Start with the first number, then add 6 to each.

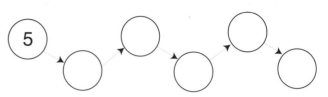

2. Work your way back along this number line, subtracting 3 each time.

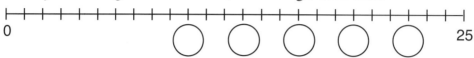

3. Complete these multiplications.

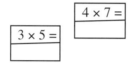

$3 \times 5 =$

$4 \times 7 =$

$5 \times 8 =$

$7 \times 9 =$

$5 \times 0 =$

4. Write 48 092 in words.

5. Fill in the missing numbers in this series.

   4835 , 4935 , [＿＿＿] , 5135 , [＿＿＿] , [＿＿＿]

6. Shade in these shapes to show $\frac{3}{4}$ on each.

7.

   $2.99 / kg $6.99 / kg

   What will it cost me for 2 kg sausages and $\frac{1}{2}$ kg bacon? [＿＿＿]

8. Circle the largest number shown on the abacuses. (a)   (b)   (c)

9. Circle the numbers which round off to ten thousand (to the nearest thousand).
   9387, 10 464, 10 509, 9872

10. I have these masses in a shopping bag; 1 × 4 kg tin, 1 × 275 g bottle, 2 kg sugar and 1 kg flour.

   I have approximately [＿＿＿] kg to carry.

Measurement and Geometry

11. 1525 hours = [＿＿＿] am / pm = [＿＿＿] past [＿＿＿]

12. Circle the objects you would measure in tonnes, and tick the ones you would measure in kilograms.

elephant, truck, train carriage, bag of oranges, bus, brick, person, dog, puppy, whale, Jumbo jet

13. Calculate the exact perimeter (in mm) of this rectangular shape.

14. Each of these shapes contains an area of 1 m². Fill in the missing dimensions.

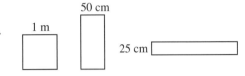

15. How many cubic centimetres of water will be needed to fill Mum's cake tray?

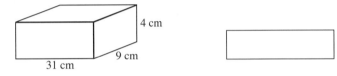

16. When I placed a thermometer in the fridge it read 3 °C. In the freezer compartment it read –8 °C. What is the difference in temperature?

17. Circle the true net of a closed cube.

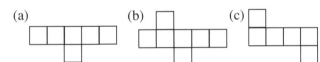

18. By inspection, which angle is 87°?

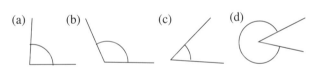

19. Which figure shows the lines of symmetry in a square?

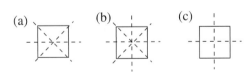

20. I'm travelling north. If I rotate 135° clockwise, I'll be travelling:

21. On a map (scale 1 : 2 000 000) the straight-line distance from Sydney to Canberra is 123 mm. What is the real distance?

Statistics and Probability

22. I have 3 coins. If they are tossed, list the possible ways (on the coins below) they can come down.

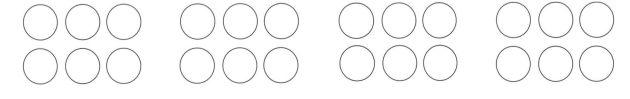

Soil salinity

Soil salinity refers to the amount of salt in the soil. If soil has too much salt it will kill any plants already growing and will not allow new plants to grow. The total area of saline soil in Australia is 3.4 per cent. Scientists estimate that a high percentage of that soil is the result of poor land management.

There are two main causes of soil salinity: irrigation and dryland. In irrigation farming, the water taken from the rivers to irrigate (water) crops usually contains salt. During irrigation, if there is more water than the crops can use, the extra water passes into the soil, picking up salt. Eventually, this water returns to the river through drainage. Over a period of time, the salt from the water builds up in the irrigation area and mixes with the salt already in the soil. Eventually, the soil becomes too salty for plant growth. This cycle of irrigation increases the amount of salt in the river. If the water is then reused for irrigation further downstream, the salinity increases to serious levels. This has happened in the Murrumbidgee irrigation area of New South Wales. A cycle has developed where the salinity of the soils and the waters of the Murray and Murrumbidgee rivers continues to increase.

The second type of salinity occurs in dryland or non-irrigated areas. It happens when trees and other vegetation are removed from hilltops, which results in more water soaking into the ground. This water collects under the ground in what is called a watertable. As the intake of water increases, the watertable further down the slope rises. As the watertable rises closer to the topsoil, the groundwater dissolves salts in the soil and forms saltpans in the valleys. Although this type of salinity occurs in patches, it is becoming more of a problem, particularly in the wheat-belt of Western Australia.

From *Technology for the Environment* by Mike Callaghan & Peter Knapp

English

Reading and Comprehension

1. Which fact about salinity is not true?
(a) Salinity will kill existing plants.
(b) Salinity will stop new plants growing.
(c) Salinity covers most of Australia.
(d) Salinity is aided by poor land management.

2. Which substance is the cause of salinity?
(a) salt
(b) soil
(c) irrigation
(d) crops

3. Saltpans result when
(a) land is covered with salty water.
(b) groundwater dissolves and raises the salt to the surface.
(c) hilltops are eroded.
(d) there is a salty watertable.

4. Over-irrigating crops increases the chance of raising salinity. True or false?

5. Though not stated, what inference can be taken from paragraph 2?
(a) The farmers need to be educated as to what causes salinity.
(b) The farmers are to blame for salinity.
(c) Salinity is a natural thing and can't be stopped.
(d) Salinity will increase no matter what is done.

Spelling and Vocabulary

Rewrite the misspelt words.

6. Sceintists are studying the salinity problem.

_____

_____

7. The Murrumbidgee irigation area in NSW has a salinity problem.

_____

_____

Circle the word that has the nearest meaning to the underlined word.

8. The topsoil becomes <u>contaminated</u>.
(a) salty
(b) polluted
(c) better
(d) more fertile

9. Salinity affects <u>3.4%</u> of Australia.
(a) 3.4 parts out of 100
(b) 3.4 parts out of 10
(c) 3.4 hectares
(d) 3.4 of the area of Australia

Circle the correct word in brackets.

10. This soil has (to, two, too) much salt in it.

11. (Their, There) is a problem to be solved.

12. The salt will (rise, raise) to the surface.

Grammar and Punctuation

13. Which of these words can't be used as nouns in sentences?

salinity, irrigation, serious, rises, saltpans

_____

_____

_____

14. Punctuate and capitalise this text.

the local mayor mr j stephens said that the salinity problem will not go away while farmers in new south wales continued to irrigate crops

_____

_____

_____

_____

_____

_____

Mathematics

Number and Algebra

1.

+	0	2	7	5	4	12
7						

2.

−	7	5	2	9	10	22
2						

3.

÷	63	54	81	36	27	90
9						

4. Write in digits: one million eight hundred and thirty-nine thousand and sixty-five.

5. Continue the pattern: 1 047 286, 1 047 288,

⬚ , ⬚

6. What fraction is unshaded?

7. Balance $562.40. Deposit $95.65.
Withdrawal $14.80.
New balance:

8. Show $\frac{35}{100}$ on this grid.

9. Round off 3 156 274 to the nearest million.

10. A number multiplied by 4 with 12 subtracted gives a result of 52. What is the number?

Measurement and Geometry

11. By knowing (longitude / latitude) we can work out time.
Write the correct word.

12. 1 kg 340 g = ⬚ kg

13. 7 m, 7 m   Perimeter = ⬚

14. Write five hectares in shortened form.

15. Write in shortened form, three cubic metres.

16. Water freezes at:

17. Draw a rectangle 4 cm long by 2 cm wide.

18. Match these angles with their names.
(a) 56°   – obtuse
(b) 108°   – reflex
(c) 203°   – acute

19. Draw in the lines of symmetry in this rectangle.

20. Give the coordinates of points A and B.

21. This is a scale drawing of a room. If the scale is 1 : 200, what are the real dimensions?

Statistics and Probability

22. This bar graph represents a total of $30. How much does Jim have?

KIM	LISA	ADRIAN	JIM

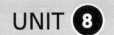

Camels and the environment

Are camels destroying the environment? Lots of other animals brought here (such as sheep, cattle, goats, cats, pigs, buffaloes, foxes and rabbits) do great damage when they run wild, so this is a good question to ask. There are no definite answers yet, but it seems that camels do not do as much damage as some of the other animals.

Camels' feet are soft pads, not the sharp hooves of animals like cattle or sheep. Camels do not eat grass much (grasses hold the soil together) but prefer to nibble at trees and shrubs. But they do seem to eat all of a particular plant that they take a great liking to, so maybe they have affected the type of plants which grow in the dry parts of Australia—they may have even wiped out some kind of plants. Camels do not form big mobs, but tend to move around in small groups. They can make waterholes all muddy and mucky, but they do not linger around them like other stock do.

From *Hoosta! The Story of Camels in Australia* by Keren Lavelle

Reading and Comprehension

1. Camels are
   (a) native.   (b) exotic.
   (c) good for Australia.   (d) important to Australia.

2. Camels' feet
   (a) cause no damage.
   (b) cause less damage than those of cattle or sheep.
   (c) cause great damage.
   (d) have soft toes.

3. Which of the following animals have not been allowed to run wild in Australia?
   (a) foxes   (b) rabbits
   (c) buffaloes   (d) dogs

4. The main food for a camel is

   _____

5. Are these sentences true or false?
   (a) Camels can damage waterholes. _____
   (b) Camels move in small groups.   _____
   (c) They eat plants they like
       before drinking.   _____
   (d) They do not remain long
       at a waterhole.   _____

Spelling and Vocabulary

Rewrite the misspelt words.

6. The lighting flashed across the night sky.

   _____

7. Seperate the good from the bad.

   _____

Circle the word that has the nearest meaning to the underlined word.

8. The Druids were <u>pagans</u>.
   (a) good fighters   (b) heathens
   (c) old   (d) Christians

9. Vitamin C will help <u>prevent</u> colds.
   (a) hinder   (b) increase   (c) many   (d) severe

Circle the correct word in brackets.

10. The tree (fell, fallen) across the track.

11. Neither Bill nor Guy (is, are) at school.

12. He should (of, have) done it.

Grammar and Punctuation

13. Give the opposite gender for the following words.

    bull   _____

    empress   _____

14. Punctuate and capitalise this sentence.

    portuguese dutch and english sailors began trading in india and china

    _____

    _____

    _____

Number and Algebra

1.

+	1	3	4	2	5	18
3						

2.

−	9	7	10	6	3	41
1						

3.

×	7	5	8	9	6	10
9						

4. What is the value of the 8 in 1 089 523?

5. Is 1 975 323 odd or even?

6. Is $\frac{15}{17}$ more or less than 1?

7. Dad's salary is $896.50 per week. Expenses $745. Savings per week =

8. Write $\frac{65}{100}$ as a decimal.

9. Give an estimate for this:

$$\begin{array}{r} 56\ 425 \\ -38\ 317 \end{array}$$

10. Find the sum of 7.56 L and 1854 mL.

Measurement and Geometry

11. One rotation of the earth takes:

12. 5624 g = ⬚ kg

13.
7 cm
3 cm

Perimeter =

14. The abbreviation *ha* stands for:

15. Which of the following would have a volume less than a cubic metre— class room, shoe box, swimming pool?

16. Water boils at ⬚ °C.

17. Construct an equilateral triangle with sides 3 cm.

18. There are ⬚ degrees in a straight angle.

19. Show the lines of symmetry in this hexagon.

20. On a grid, is (3, 5) the same point as (5, 3)?

21. Here is the road from A to B. The scale is 1 cm = 5 km. How far is town A from B?

A

B

Statistics and Probability

22. These makes of cars were owned by families of 6T.

Holden	Ford	Toyota

Which make of car is the most popular?

Tower Hill

Since 1961 hundreds of schoolchildren have planted 250 000 trees and shrubs on Tower Hill. This cone-shaped hill, north of Warrnambool in western Victoria, can be seen from the sea.

Thousands of years ago, Tower Hill was a volcano. When the top of the hill blasted away, a crater was left. Early last century, white explorers came. They saw a crater, partly filled with water. There were three forested islands with a variety of wildlife.

In 1857, settlers began to fell the timber on the slopes of the crater and on the islands. They wanted to clear the land for grazing sheep. Eight years later, the trees were gone, and the slopes were covered with bracken and grass. Wild animals and birds had disappeared.

Later, vegetables were grown on the banks of the lake, and stones were quarried from the crater. Early this century, the lake was almost dry, and cattle were grazed there. Very little of the original vegetation (plant life) was left.

From *Saving Wildlife* by Edel Wignell

Reading and Comprehension

1. Tower Hill was originally a
    (a) volcano.   (b) crater.
    (c) cone-shaped hill.   (d) lake.

2. Settlers began timber clearing there
    (a) in 1961.
    (b) in 1857.
    (c) thousands of years ago.
    (d) early last century.

3. The purpose of timber clearing was to
    (a) get rid of the wild animals and birds.
    (b) grow vegetables.
    (c) graze sheep.
    (d) quarry for stone.

4. By which year had all the trees gone?

_____

5. Number these sentences in order (1–4).
    (a) Many wild creatures lived on Tower Hill.
    (b) Very little water was left in the lake.
    (c) A volcanic explosion once occurred there.
    (d) Cattle grazed in this area.

Spelling and Vocabulary

Rewrite the misspelt words.

6. Vegtables are good for you.

_____

7. I heard the terrable sound coming from the room.

_____

Circle the word that has the nearest meaning to the underlined word.

8. The eagle used its <u>talons</u> to hold its prey.
    (a) feathers   (b) beak
    (c) wings   (d) claws

9. The lake appeared <u>serene</u> in the early morning.
    (a) calm   (b) beautiful
    (c) cold   (d) inviting

Circle the correct word in brackets.

10. This can be done (easy, easily).

11. They have (went, gone) by train.

12. None of the goods (is, are) missing.

Grammar and Punctuation

13. Join these sentences. Don't use the word *and*.

The refugees had no clothing. They had no food. The refugees had no water.

_____

_____

14. Punctuate and capitalise this sentence.

the nrma helps many motorists in new south wales

_____

_____

Number and Algebra

1.

+	7	8	6	4	2	14
0						

2.

−	15	12	7	14	9	66
6						

3.

÷	18	24	12	15	21	39
3						

4. Arrange in ascending order.
1 056 923 , 1 059 632 , 1 059 623

5. Count on from 2 101 085, 2 101 090,

6. One (1) can be broken into [ ]
fifteenths.

7. Find the total. Onions $1.59, potatoes $2.99,
carrots 79c, beans $2.20,
cucumber 59c, garlic $3.57. [ ]

8. Convert $\frac{15}{20}$ to a decimal. [ ]

9. Round off 7513 g to
the nearest kg. [ ]

10. Metal sheet is 1.2 mm thick. How many
sheets must be put together
to have a thickness of
1.44 cm? [ ]

Measurement and Geometry

11. One hour difference is given
by (360°, 15° or 1°) rotation
of the earth. [ ]

12. Container 85 g, contents 370 g
Total mass = [ ]

13. Measure each side and calculate the perimeter.

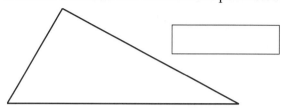

[ ]

14. Circle the area I would measure in hectares.
school grounds / classroom / page in pad / farm

15. Which of these would have a volume greater
than a cubic metre? Circle your answer.
kitchen / drawer / office

16. Show 39 °C on this thermometer.

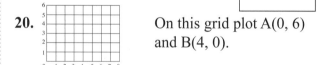

0°   10°   20°   30°   40°   50°

17. Construct a square
with sides of 15 mm. [ ]

18. A full rotation is [ ] degrees.

19. Use your compass within
this shape to create a
symmetrical pattern. [ ]

20. On this grid plot A(0, 6)
and B(4, 0).

21. A paddock is 38 m
long and 14 m wide.
Draw this to the
scale of 1 : 1000. [ ]

Statistics and Probability

22. Draw this tally of pets
in our class on a bar graph [ ]

Dogs ||||| ||||| ||||| |
Cats ||||| |||
Birds ||||| |

Do cats and birds together
form a greater
fraction of pets? [ ]

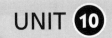

The truth about tooth decay

We now know that caries is caused by the bacteria in our saliva. Some bacteria actually do look like tiny worms: so tiny that you need a powerful microscope to see them at all. But bacteria are not tiny worms, so the ancient civilizations who believed in the toothworm were on the wrong track.

On a piece of scrap paper, draw a circle one centimetre in diameter. Now, if you were to spit on that circle, that little pool of saliva would contain *at least* one million bacteria. Your saliva keeps washing over your teeth, coating them with a thin, jelly-like film called plaque. This is the acid, gummy substance that forms on teeth between cleanings. Bacteria then develop in the plaque and eat away at your teeth. This is why you need to brush your teeth after meals.

Bacteria are the enemy! They attack the gums as well as the teeth.

From *The Tooth Book* by Viki Wright

Reading and Comprehension

1. Bacteria
    (a) are tiny worms.
    (b) appear to be tiny worms.
    (c) act like worms.
    (d) are really toothworms.

2. Teeth should be brushed
    (a) regularly.
    (b) every day.
    (c) after meals.
    (d) to remove saliva.

3. Which of the following is the real enemy of teeth and gums?
    (a) spit   (b) plaque
    (c) saliva   (d) bacteria

4. What does the word *caries* mean?

    _____

5. Number these sentences in order (1–4).
    (a) Plaque forms on teeth.
    (b) Bacteria destroys teeth and gums.
    (c) Saliva contains plaque.
    (d) Bacteria develops in plaque.

Spelling and Vocabulary

Rewrite the misspelt words.

6. Grandad made a woden rocking hoarse.

    _____

7. Self-raising flower is needed for this recipe.

    _____

Circle the word that has the nearest meaning to the underlined word.

8. His dog has a good <u>pedigree</u>.
    (a) ancestral line   (b) coat
    (c) bark   (d) bite

9. Dina plays the <u>marimba</u>.
    (a) trumpet
    (b) African xylophone
    (c) Spanish guitar
    (d) South American cymbals

Circle the correct word in brackets.

10. Mr Smith (taught, learned) me to read.

11. I waited (upon, for) her for 10 minutes.

12. The sun had (rose, risen) by six am.

Grammar and Punctuation

13. Underline the adjectives in the following sentence.

    The lean, hungry lion prepared to spring onto the unsuspecting, plump warthog.

14. Punctuate and capitalise this sentence.

    kate said that she went to katoomba last sunday

    _____

    _____

Number and Algebra

1.

+	5	8	6	7	9	16
4						

2.

−	3	5	8	0	6	13
0						

3.

×	2	5	3	6	4	11
7						

4. Arrange in descending order.
1 011 011, 1 101 010, 1 100 111

5. Count backwards from 1 009 000 in 5000s.

               ,

6. To be greater than 1, the numerator is (greater than / less than) the denominator.

7. Meat $17.60, groceries $22.65, fruit $12.95. Total:

8. Use your calculator to find $\frac{3}{7}$ as a decimal.

9. Round off to the nearest ten cents and add $26.24, $35.39 and $14.25.

10. What is the total length when 1.68 m, 732 mm and 596 cm are added?

Measurement and Geometry

11. It's 9 am in Sydney (150°E). What's the time in Tokyo (150°E)?

12. Carton 425 g, contents $3\frac{1}{2}$ kg

     Total mass =

13. Find the perimeter of a rectangle 5 cm long and 30 mm wide.

14. Convert 20 000 m² to hectares.

15. A shop has a volume of 2250 (metres / square metres / cubic metres). Choose the correct unit.

16. Name the instrument used to measure temperature.

17. Describe how you could draw a circle on the ground with a radius of 5 m.

18. Write 75 ° in full form.

19. Use your compass with the points set at the radius of this circle, to create a symmetrical pattern.

20. Name the corners of this triangle.

A (,   )
B (,   )
C (,   )

21. A garden is 20 m long and 14 m wide. If I draw it to a scale of 1 : 100, my drawing will

be   long and   wide.

Statistics and Probability

22. This bar graph shows the favourite sports of 20 children.

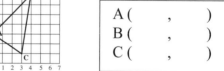

Netball	Soccer	Tennis	Soft-ball

Approximately how many children play tennis and softball?

Reading maps

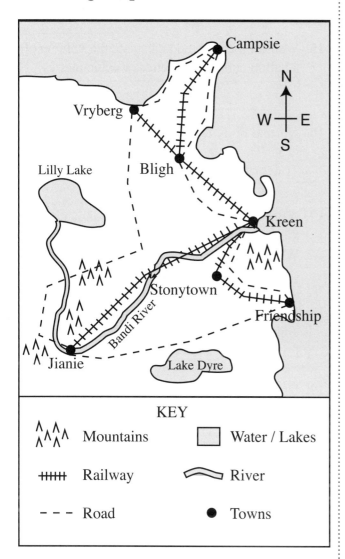

KEY

⋀⋀⋀ Mountains   ☐ Water / Lakes

╫╫╫ Railway   ⌒ River

- - - Road   ● Towns

Reading and Comprehension

1. Between which two towns is the longest stretch of railway?

_____

2. Is it further from Vryberg to Kreen than Campsie to Kreen?

_____

3. In which general direction would you travel if you were to fly from Campsie to Bligh?

_____

4. Which lake is south of Stonytown and east of Jianie?

_____

5. On which trip would you cross a river, pass through mountains and travel in a north-easterly direction?

_____

Spelling and Vocabulary

Rewrite the misspelt words.

6. The sun peeped over the horison.

_____

7. The boarder between Victoria and New South Wales is the Murray River.

_____

Circle the word that has the nearest meaning to the underlined word.

8. He delivered his speech from the <u>lectern</u>.
   (a) stage   (b) tall desk
   (c) table   (d) audience

9. Vlad, the impaler, was a <u>despot</u>.
   (a) good ruler   (b) tyrant
   (c) bad ruler   (d) democratic ruler

Circle the correct word in brackets.

10. A kangaroo (have, has) a long tail.

11. Here (is, are) some grapes for you.

12. Everyone should (be, been) honest.

Grammar and Punctuation

13. Write the singular form of the following words.

oxen   _____   lice   _____

babies   _____

14. Punctuate and capitalise this sentence.

after john recited the man from snowy river mary sang waltzing matilda

_____

_____

Number and Algebra

1.

+	7	3	2	8	4	19
9						

2.

–	10	13	14	11	12	34
5						

3.

÷	32	8	36	16	28	88
4						

4. Write 1 649 093 in words.

5. Count on from 985 147 in ten thousands.

⬚ , ⬚

6. Write the fraction with 29 as the numerator and 50 as the denominator.

7. Find the total: bus fares $6.20, lunches $7.10, entertainment $9.60.

8. Convert $\frac{56}{100}$ to a percentage.

9. 49% of $32.00 is roughly:

Measurement and Geometry

10. Two different rectangles have the same perimeter. Are their areas equal?

11. How many seconds in 20 minutes?

12. 4 kg of water has a volume of ⬚ L.

13. A square with a side of 10 cm has a perimeter of 100 cm or 1 metre. True or false?

14. 1.56 ha = ⬚ m²

15. Would I measure and calculate the volume of a ball in cubic centimetres or cubic metres?

16. Normal body temperature is 37 °C. True or false?

17. A big water pipe has an internal diameter of 85 cm and an external diameter of 97 cm. What is the thickness of the pipe wall?

18. Write one hundred and eight degrees in shortened form.

19. Draw the lines of symmetry in this shape.

20. Name the direction midway between South and West.

21. On a map (scale 1 : 100 000) the distance between Toogood and Lettyville is 19 mm. What is the real distance between the two towns?

Statistics and Probability

22. This graph shows the rainfall in Darwin. Which month would be:
(a) least likely to have a wet day?
(b) most likely to have a wet day?

J F M A M J J A S O N D

The birthplace of kites

Kites have been flown in China since about 400 BC: around the time when work began on the Great Wall of China.

Chinese kites were often used for military purposes. One of the earliest accounts tell how a general, Han Xian, was trying to invade a heavily guarded palace. He flew a kite over the wall of the palace, then measured the length of the kite string to calculate the distance required to reach the inside of the palace.

Using the measurement as a guide, Han Xian tunnelled secretly under the wall of the palace and took the defenders by surprise.

During the Han Dynasty (202 BC–AD 220) kites were also used in battle, to scare the enemy. They were fitted with hummers made from bamboo pipes. These made eerie sounds as the kites flew over sleeping soldiers in their camps.

The soldiers would awake terrified at the sound of mysterious attacking monsters and flee their camp, leaving their weapons and belongings behind.

From *Kites* by David Bowden & Jenny Dibley

Reading and Comprehension

1. Kites were first flown in China
   (a) 400 years ago.
   (b) 400 years before the birth of Christ.
   (c) 400 years after the birth of Christ.
   (d) for 400 years.

2. What caused the hummers on kites to make eerie sounds?
   (a) the kite   (b) the bamboo
   (c) the enemy   (d) the wind

3. Han Xian
   (a) liked flying kites.
   (b) was the first to fly a kite.
   (c) flew kites for military purposes.
   (d) flew kites over cities.

4. Name the construction which began in China around the time when kites were first flown.
   _____

5. Number these sentences in order (1–4).
   (a) By knowing the length of string he could work out the distance.
   (b) The palace was taken by surprise.
   (c) Han Xian flew his kite over the palace wall.
   (d) The defenders did not expect Han Xian's men to tunnel into the palace.

Spelling and Vocabulary

Rewrite the misspelt words.

6. Gold is a very good conducter of electricity.
   _____

7. The refridgerator is too cold.
   _____

Circle the word that has the nearest meaning to the underlined word.

8. Juvenile plants need extra care.
   (a) young   (b) old   (c) green   (d) sprouting

9. I was amazed by the judge's lenient sentence.
   (a) mild   (b) severe
   (c) appropriate   (d) fair

Circle the correct word in brackets.

10. Bill is (tall, taller) than Sam.

11. Will you (skin, peel) the orange?

12. The shoe is (warn, worn) out.

Grammar and Punctuation

13. Write a sentence using *match* as a noun.
    _____
    _____

14. Punctuate and capitalise this sentence.

    whispering springs is a homestead on the banks of the darling river
    _____
    _____
    _____

Number and Algebra

1.

+	2	9	4	3	8	49
1						

2.

–	5	8	6	11	7	53
4						

3.

×	2	0	7	3	5	18
2						

4. Write one number for
1 000 000 + 600 000 + 50 000
+ 9000 + 600 + 9.

5. Is 6.3 (odd / even / neither)?

6. Write the fraction for 15
out of 24 equal parts.

7. From an income of $346.90, $275.35 was
spent, leaving $ [ ] for savings.

8. 0.8 as a percentage is:

9. 9.95% is very close to
(0.1 / 1.0 / 0.9).

10. A can is 90% full. If it holds
20 L when full, how much
is in the can?

Measurement and Geometry

11. How many minutes
in $3\frac{1}{2}$ hours?

12. 3000 mL of water has a mass of
[ ] kg.

13. Measure the dimensions accurately and
calculate the perimeter.

Perimeter =

14. A hectare must be a square
measuring 100 m on each
side. True or false?

15. Write fifty-one cubic metres
in shortened form.

16. Match these temperatures and places.
(a) Snowy Mountains (winter)   20 °C
(b) Alice Springs (summer)   – 14 °C
(c) Sydney (spring)   35 °C

17. On this circle name the:
(a) centre
(b) diameter
(c) radius
(d) circumference

18. What is the size
of this angle?

19. How many lines of symmetry can
be drawn in a scalene
triangle?

20. A wind blowing from the West towards the
East is called a [ ] wind.

21. Our NRMA map has a scale of 1 cm : 20 km.
Canowindra is 12 cm (in a straight line)
from Sydney. So by plane from Sydney to
Canowindra is [ ] km.

Statistics and Probability

22. Draw this information onto the pie graph.
$\frac{2}{6}$ carrots, $\frac{1}{6}$ tomatoes,

$\frac{1}{6}$ beans, $\frac{2}{6}$ potatoes

Puppets

In the earliest recorded times puppets, like other forms of theatre, such as plays and dance, were used not only to entertain, but as a way of teaching people about their religion, their culture and their history. This was most important, as at that time hardly anybody knew how to read or write.

In some countries today puppets are still used to tell traditional stories, but often they are used solely to entertain. A few modern puppets, especially those seen by large audiences on television, have become extremely popular. Nearly everyone will have seen some of the characters created by puppeteer Jim Henson, whose Muppets appear regularly on a variety of programmes, and have even starred in their own movies. Although a puppet is not strictly a doll, the name does come from the Latin word for doll, *puppa*. Unlike a doll, a puppet is animated or brought to life by the puppeteer who moves it by pulling strings, pushing it on a rod, or placing a hand inside the puppet's body.

From *Puppets* by Carole Hooper

Reading and Comprehension

1. Which of the following methods are not used for puppets' movements?
   (a) hand inside the puppet
   (b) pulling strings
   (c) moving rods
   (d) hand holding onto the puppet

2. Early puppet shows were used
   (a) to entertain.
   (b) to teach.
   (c) for religious purposes.
   (d) to teach and entertain.

3. Puppets were originally created because
   (a) people needed to be entertained.
   (b) television was popular.
   (c) few could read or write.
   (d) people wanted to learn about theatre.

4. From which language does the word *puppet* come? _____

5. Number these sentences in order (1–4).
   (a) Puppets like the Muppets are meant to entertain.
   (b) Puppets do still tell traditional stories.
   (c) Puppets were meant to educate people.
   (d) People learned about their historical, cultural and religious development through puppets.

Spelling and Vocabulary

Rewrite the misspelt words.

6. My adress is written on this envelope.

   _____

7. The biscut has currants and sultanas in it.

   _____

Circle the word that has the nearest meaning to the underlined word.

8. I need Dad's underline{approbation} before I go.
   (a) approval   (b) blessing
   (c) applause   (d) best wishes

9. "Please don't underline{chide} me", she said.
   (a) help   (b) scold   (c) hit   (d) disturb

Circle the correct word in brackets.

10. He was carrying a heavy (load, cargo).

11. The dentist will (haul, pull) out my aching tooth.

12. The bank has been (hurt, damaged) by the floodwaters.

Grammar and Punctuation

13. Change this sentence so that it refers to the future.

    He stood beside the door.

    _____

14. Punctuate and capitalise this sentence.

    i read an interesting story about elvis presley in mums womans day magazine

    _____

    _____

    _____

Number and Algebra

1.

+	5	8	6	9	7	16
5						

2.

−	16	18	10	17	12	99
9						

3.

÷	6	7	5	1	2	99
1						

4. Expand 2 583 264.

5. Give the next number:

900 549 , 950 549 ,

6. Show $\frac{5}{9}$ by shading in this rectangle.

7. If $3856.25 is withdrawn from a balance of $7313.10, then ____ remains.

8. $\frac{47}{50} = \frac{\square}{100} = 0.\square = \square$ %

9. Round off 3 552 152 to the nearest hundred thousand.

10. A number divided by 3 with 19 added equals 36. What is the number?

Measurement and Geometry

11. I run for 30 minutes each day. How many hours do I run in a week?

12. A bucket is 720 g. If $5\frac{1}{2}$ litres of water are added, the total mass equals:

13. Which has the greater perimeter?

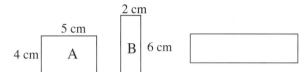

14.

1000 m

10 m

Calculate the area in hectares.

15. Circle the greater volume.
48 725 cm³   or 1 m³

16. Generally speaking, as you travel south, temperature (increases / decreases).

17. In a circle the diameter is ____ the length of the radius.

18. Which is the larger angle: 175° or a reflex angle?

19. Draw the line of symmetry in this isosceles triangle.

20. If ↓ is North then ↗ is:

21. Which would be the larger map of Australia?
(a) 1 cm : 25 km
(b) 1 cm : 80 km

Statistics and Probability

22. This pie graph represents a day in Jean's life.

At school, Sleeping, Eating, Playing

What fraction of the day is spent playing?

Japan

Japan's capital city, Tokyo, is the largest city in the world with a population of more than 18 million. Japan is a scenic country with snow-capped mountains, peach blossoms in spring, and many formal rock gardens. It is also one of the most industrialised nations and produces household consumer goods known to most Australians. Japan's total population is now near 123 million.

Four major islands make up Japan: Honshu, Hokkaido, Kyushu and Shikoku. Parts of Japan are overcrowded. There are contrasts between exciting neon-lit cities like Tokyo, to volcanic peaks like Mount Fuji, shimmering green rice paddies, and the busy industrial coastal ports. The country is dotted with religious shrines and temples as religion plays an important part in Japanese life.

The key to Japanese food is its freshness. Even with the introduction of refrigeration many Japanese will shop daily to buy the freshest ingredients for cooking. Unlike other Asian food most Japanese food is not spicy; the sparseness of seasoning is unique.

From *What's Cooking* by Kerrie Bingle et al.

Reading and Comprehension

1. How many islands make up the country of Japan?
   (a) 4 only   (b) more than 4
   (c) less than 4   (d) 18 million

2. Tokyo has a population
   (a) similar to the whole of Australia.
   (b) of 123 million.
   (c) less than Australia.
   (d) much greater than Australia.

3. Japanese food is
   (a) not spicy.   (b) usually bought daily.
   (c) refrigerated.   (d) as fresh as possible.
   (Select the one which is not true.)

4. Which word implies that there are numerous shrines and temples in Japan? _____

5. The passage says Japan is a land of contrasts because
   (a) it is made up of islands.
   (b) there are many shrines and temples.
   (c) the food is different to other Asian countries.
   (d) it has quiet countryside and busy cities.

Spelling and Vocabulary

Rewrite the misspelt words.

6. We are going across the Simpson Dessert.

   _____

7. Febuary is the second month of the year.

   _____

Circle the word that has the nearest meaning to the underlined word.

8. Don't <u>dally</u> on your way home.
   (a) run   (b) stop
   (c) dawdle   (d) talk to strangers

9. Spanish people enjoy a <u>fiesta</u>.
   (a) alcoholic drink (b) party (c) festival (d) dance

Circle the correct word in brackets.

10. The mosquitoes (teased, annoyed) me.

11. (There, Their) they are.

12. Read (these, them) sentences carefully.

Grammar and Punctuation

13. Join these sentences into one (don't use *and*).

    The lion will not go to the spring. The moon is shining. He will be easily seen.

    _____

    _____

14. Punctuate and capitalise this sentence.

    near the entrance to the cave jenna found dutch english and spanish coins

    _____

    _____

Number and Algebra

1.

+	3	6	4	7	5	36
6						

2.

−	8	10	7	2	9	80
1						

3.

×	6	5	9	7	8	14
4						

4. Circle the larger number: 1 047 073, 1 074 037

5. What number is 10 000 less than 1 million?

6. Show $\frac{7}{8}$ on this shape.

7. How much will I have if I add $70.69 to my balance of $183.27?

8. Find 26% of $1.

9. Estimate, then check, the length of this line segment.

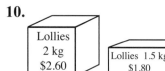

10. Which is the better buy?

Lollies 2 kg $2.60
Lollies 1.5 kg $1.80

Measurement and Geometry

11. London is 0°. Sydney is on 150°E. So Sydney is 10 hours (ahead of / behind) London.

12. 7256 mL of water has a mass of

kg.

13. Measure the dimensions of this triangle and calculate the perimeter.

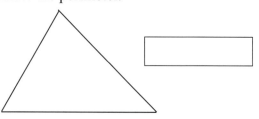

14. Sydney Harbour is (more / less) than 1 hectare.

15. A shipping container has a volume (greater / less) than 1 m³.

16. It was 27 °C today. Overnight the temperature will fall 11° to

.

17. Use your compass to draw a circle which has a diameter of 1.4 cm.

18. In a full rotation there are   right angles.

19. Complete this shape based on the line of symmetry.

20.

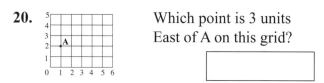

Which point is 3 units East of A on this grid?

21. A tree is 5.4 m high. If it is drawn to a scale of 1 : 100, the drawing will be   tall.

Statistics and Probability

22. Read the information on the pie graph showing votes for TV programs.

(a) What percentage of votes did Quiz receive?

(b) How many more per cent of the vote did Quiz gain over News?

Mars

Mars, the fourth planet out from the Sun, is the last of the rocky planets. Mars is about half the size of our Earth and takes about 23 months to loop around the Sun. A day on Mars is only 41 minutes longer than a day on Earth. Mars is about 6780 km across. At the centre is an iron core about 3000 km across. This iron core is covered by a rocky mantle about 1800 km thick. Right at the surface is the crust, which is about 100 km thick. Although Mars does not have much gas in its atmosphere, it does have weather. The winds, which can last for months at a time, blow at speeds of up to 350 km per hour. In many of the canyons found on Mars there are fogs in the early morning, and in the afternoon clouds form around some of the mountains.

The north and south poles on Mars shrink in the summer and expand in the winter. They are made of water-ice and dry ice (solid carbon dioxide). There is no flowing water on Mars, however there are many channels on the planet which look just like dried-up river beds and scientists believe that many millions of years ago there must have been water on Mars. Some scientists believe that there could be lots of water just under the surface of Mars and that life could survive in this water.

From Spacescape by Karl Kruszelnicki

Reading and Comprehension

1. A year on Mars is equal to
   (a) almost two earth years.   (b) 41 minutes.
   (c) 24 hours 41 minutes.   (d) one year.

2. If you were able to dig to the core of Mars, you would pass through
   (a) core, mantle, crust.
   (b) crust, mantle, core.
   (c) crust, core, mantle.
   (d) mantle, crust, core.

3. Based on the details in this extract, the diameter of Earth is
   (a) 6780 km.   (b) 3000 km.
   (c) 13 000 km.   (d) 3000 + 1800 + 100 km.

4. Name at least two weather conditions found on Mars.

_____

5. Which statement indicates that there once was water on Mars?
   (a) The poles expand and contract depending on the season.
   (b) There is water under the surface.
   (c) The channels look as though they were formed by flowing water.
   (d) To have had life, Mars must have had water once.

Spelling and Vocabulary

Rewrite the misspelt words.

6. He guest the answer. _____

7. I borrowed a good book from the local libary.

_____

Circle the word that has the nearest meaning to the underlined word.

8. Mike has a wonderful <u>numismatic</u> collection.
   (a) bird   (b) stamp
   (c) card   (d) coin

9. Some monkeys have a <u>prehensile</u> tail.
   (a) long   (b) short
   (c) can hold onto things   (d) long and fluffy

Circle the correct word in brackets.

10. Did you read (those, them) books?

11. He is (write, right) handed.

12. Sit (here, hear) and wait.

Grammar and Punctuation

13. Place the correct ending on the word *tall* to fit this sentence.

   She is the _____ girl I've ever seen.

14. Punctuate and capitalise this sentence.

   werent you at taronga park zoo last saturday meeka

_____

_____

Mathematics

Number and Algebra

1. Complete these.

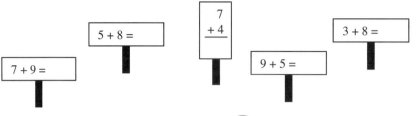

2. Find answers to these.

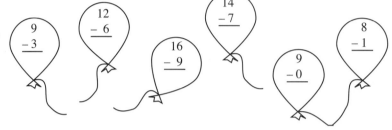

3. Give answers to these.

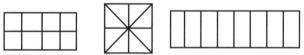

4. Expand 4 090 719.

5. Complete this series. 935 872 , 955 872 , 975 872 , [   ] , [   ] .

6. On each of these shapes show $\frac{5}{8}$.

7. On 15 June I had $92.87. After that I made some deposits and some withdrawals. My balance now is $113.54 which means my deposits are (greater / less) than my withdrawals by $ [   ]

8. Shade in to show 60%.

9. Estimate which line segment is closer to 87 mm.
   (a) _____
   (b) _____
   (c) _____

10. A drip (1 mL) comes from a tap every 10 seconds.
How much water will be wasted in one day?

Measurement and Geometry

11. Mel plays squash for an hour on Mondays and Wednesdays, and two hours on Saturdays. How many hours does she play in two weeks?

Answers

Maths

1. 12, 13, 11, 7, 14, 21
2. 2, 1, 9, 3, 6, 26
3. 72, 16, 32, 48, 56, 96
4. 37 861
5. 169, 171, 173
6. 1.4
7. $34.55
8.
9. 190 000
10. 1×$20, 1×$10, 2×$2, 1×50c, 1×20c, 1×10c, 1×5c
11. 7:50 pm
12. find own mass, hold dog in arms, find new mass, then subtract for mass of dog
13. 24 mm
14. 24 m²
15. 24
16. 45 °C
17. square-based pyramid
18. 90°, 180°
19. 20.
21. 55 cm
22. 1, 2, 3, 4, 5 or 6

English

1. b
2. d
3. a
4. Persia
5. 1b, 2d, 3a, 4c
6. bandage
7. answer, correct
8. b
9. b
10. were
11. have
12. was
13. Bass, Flinders, Sydney, *Tom Thumb*
14. He muttered, "It isn't fair."

Maths

1. 10, 7, 11, 8, 9, 21
2. 9, 1, 7, 3, 5, 28
3. 3, 1, 4, 2, 6, 9
4. forty-seven thousand one hundred and ninety-eight
5. 2048, 2050, 2052
6.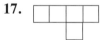
7. 1×$20, 1×$10, 1×$2, 1×$1, 1×50c, 1×5c
8. 3.62
9. 56 800
10. 10.68
11. 12:05 pm
12. 275 g
13. 66 mm
14. 2.25 m²
15. 60
16. − 17°C
17.
18. acute
19. A -B -C -D -E -F G H
20. b
21. 1.6 m
22. 2

English

1. d
2. c
3. b
4. To give a peace-offering to his master.
5. 1b, 2c, 3d, 4a
6. startle
7. mystery
8. c
9. d
10. are
11. he
12. I
13. He went to herd the sheep into the pen.
14. "Where are you going?" asked Jim.

Maths

1. 8, 15, 11, 13, 17, 25
2. 4, 8, 2, 6, 0, 36
3. 6, 21, 9, 24, 18, 36
4. 6000
5. 12, 17, 23
6. $\frac{2}{5}$
7. $156.95
8. 2 tenths
9. 8 m
10. $1125
11. 1303 hours
12. 755 g
13. 10.5 cm
14. 5712 m²
15. 5 cm
16. 19°
17. false
18. 150°
19. 20. (D, 10)
21. 38 mm
22. 74

English

1. c
2. b
3. a
4. Hey, Hey It's Saturday
5. 1b, 2c, 3d, 4a
6. brilliant
7. procession
8. b
9. b
10. grown
11. rang
12. written
13. I did my work on time.
14. You'll find that there's more gold here than we've ever seen.

Answers

ANSWERS: *Excel* Basic Skills English and Mathematics Year 6

UNIT 4 page 14

Maths

1. 12, 11, 14, 17, 15, 20
2. 5, 7, 3, 6, 2, 24
3. 8, 4, 7, 2, 3, 6
4.
5. 12, 14, 15
6. 12.14
7. $17.25
8. 2.74
9. 2 L
10. 44 640
11. 2:25 am, 0225 hours
12. 8.07 t
13. metres
14. convert measurements to same units
15. cube
16. − 7°
17. 4
18. reflex
19.   20. east
21. 1 mm
22. 36

English

1. a
2. d
3. d
4. true
5. 1b, 2d, 3a, 4c
6. purpose
7. competition
8. b
9. d
10. sprang
11. nor
12. than
13. A crow was thirsty so he flew to the tank hoping that there would be water in it. (or similar)
14. "It's a flock of emus," stated Ken.

UNIT 5 page 16

Maths

1. 5, 11, 9, 10, 4, 22
2. 1, 8, 3, 5, 6, 18
3. 30, 0, 6, 36, 54, 60
4. 625 428
5. 680, 675, 670
6. $\dfrac{16}{20}$
7. $2.80
8. 7, 3, 5
9. 8 hours
10. 1026.3 km
11. 11:45 am, 1145 hours
12. tonnes
13. 154 mm, 15.4 cm
14. false
15. 96 cm³
16. 37 °C
17. 12
18. 32°
19. an infinite number
20. south-east
21. check drawing, 3 cm long, 1.5 cm wide
22. 130

English

1. d
2. a
3. c
4. iron/steel
5. 1b, 2d, 3a, 4c
6. brother
7. currant
8. b
9. a
10. quay
11. allowed
12. coarse
13. wives, gases, sheep
14. You'll have to travel along Jones Road till you come to Wilsons Crossing.

UNIT 6 page 18

Maths

1. 8, 6, 1, 7, 10, 30
2. 5, 3, 1, 9, 7, 40
3. 5, 9, 3, 7, 1, 24
4. 100 000 + 60 000 + 8000 + 500 + 70 + 4
5. 1195, 1095, 995
6. $\dfrac{3}{8}$
7. $888.55
8. 7
9. 4981, 4819, 4918
10. 317 440
11. 1:46 pm
12. same
13. 64 cm
14. b
15. 72 cm³
16. 46°
17. sphere
18. 315°
19.
20. south-west
21. 16 m
22. 1 blue, 1 green, 6 red; or 2 blue, 2 green, 4 red

English

1. d
2. b
3. a
4. 4°
5. 1b, 2d, 3a, 4c
6. Two
7. fort
8. b
9. a
10. pale
11. beach
12. broken
13. from
14. "The pup," said the farmer's wife, "is hungry."

Answers

Maths

1. 8, 13, 10, 6, 14, 30
2. 7, 8, 5, 3, 6, 40
3. 20, 30, 10, 15, 40, 50
4. 265 976
5. 8164, 9164, 10 164
6.
7. $2776.75
8. 8
9. 10 000 to nearest thousand
10. 1365
11. 1915 hours
12. weight of plastic bag
13. 22 cm
14. 10 cm²
15. 200
16. 48 °C
17. true
18. protractor
19. [diagram] 20. [compass diagram]
21. 3.2 km
22. 105

English

1. (a) 2 hours 55 minutes
   (b) 8 hours 55 minutes
2. 73 minutes, or 1 hour and 13 minutes
3. Albury to Goulburn, or Benalla to Harden, or Wangaratta to Yass Junction
4. Cootamundra
5. 10 hours 45 minutes
6. Here's
7. practise
8. d
9. a
10. tracked
11. straight
12. paced
13. The deer was hunted by the dogs.
14. Mr AL Jones helped Ms TA Smith with her speech.

Maths

1. 11, 17, 23, 29, 35
2. 22, 19, 16, 13, 10
3. 15, 28, 40, 63, 0
4. forty-eight thousand and ninety-two
5. 5035, 5235, 5335
6.
7. $9.50 to nearest 5c
8. a
9. 10 464, 9872
10. 7 kg
11. 3:25 pm, 25 past 3
12. tonnes: elephant, truck, train carriage, bus, whale, Jumbo jet.
    kilograms: bag of oranges, brick, person, dog, puppy.
13. 182 mm
14. 1 m, 2 m, 4 m
15. 1116 cm³
16. 11°
17. c
18. a
19. b
20. south-east
21. 246 km
22. HHH, HTH, HHT, HTT, TTT, THT, TTH, THH

English

1. c
2. a
3. b
4. true
5. a
6. scientists
7. irrigation
8. b
9. a
10. too
11. There
12. rise
13. serious, rises
14. The local Mayor, Mr J Stephens, said that the salinity problem will not go away while farmers in New South Wales continued to irrigate crops.

Maths

1. 7, 9, 14, 12, 11, 19
2. 5, 3, 0, 7, 8, 20
3. 7, 6, 9, 4, 3, 10
4. 1 839 065
5. 1 047 290, 1 047 292
6. $\dfrac{7}{12}$
7. $643.25
8. shade in 35 squares
9. 3 000 000
10. 16
11. longitude
12. 1.340
13. 28 m
14. 5 ha
15. 3 m³
16. 0 °C
17. check measurements
18. a-acute, b-obtuse, c-reflex
19. [diagram]
20. (3, 3), (5, 6)
21. 5.2 m long × 3.6 m wide
22. $7.50

English

1. b
2. b
3. d
4. trees and shrubs
5. True, true, false, true
6. lightning
7. Separate
8. b
9. a
10. fell
11. is
12. have
13. cow, emperor
14. Portuguese, Dutch and English sailors began trading in India and China.

Answers

UNIT 9 page 28

Maths

1. 4, 6, 7, 5, 8, 21
2. 8, 6, 9, 5, 2, 40
3. 63, 45, 72, 81, 54, 90
4. 80 000
5. odd
6. less
7. $151.50
8. 0.65
9. 20 000
10. 9.414 L
11. 24 hours
12. 5.624 kg
13. 20 cm
14. hectares
15. shoe box
16. 100 °C
17. check drawing
18. 180°
19.
20. no
21. 35 km
22. Holden

English

1. a
2. b
3. c
4. 1865
5. 1c, 2a, 3d, 4b
6. vegetables
7. terrible
8. d
9. a
10. easily
11. gone
12. is
13. The refugees had no food, clothes or water. (or similar)
14. The NRMA helps many motorists in New South Wales.

UNIT 10 page 30

Maths

1. 7, 8, 6, 4, 2, 14
2. 9, 6, 1, 8, 3, 60
3. 6, 8, 4, 5, 7, 13
4. 1 056 923, 1 059 623, 1 059 632
5. 2 101 095, 2 101 100, 2 101 105
6. 15
7. $11.73
8. 0.75
9. 8 kg
10. 12
11. 15°
12. 455 g
13. 146 mm
14. school grounds, farm
15. kitchen, office
16.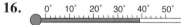
17. check drawing
18. 360°
19. 20.
    or similar
21. check drawing
22. no

English

1. b
2. c
3. d
4. holes/cavities
5. 1c, 2a, 3d, 4b
6. wooden, horse
7. flour
8. a
9. b
10. taught
11. for
12. risen
13. lean, hungry, unsuspecting, plump
14. Kate said that she went to Katoomba last Sunday.

UNIT 11 page 32

Maths

1. 9, 12, 10, 11, 13, 20
2. 3, 5, 8, 0, 6, 13
3. 14, 35, 21, 42, 28, 77
4. 1 101 010, 1 100 111, 1 011 011
5. 1 004 000, 999 000
6. greater than
7. $53.20
8. 0.428 5714
9. $75.90
10. 8.372 m
11. 9 am
12. 3.925 kg
13. 16 cm
14. 2 ha
15. m³
16. thermometer
17. peg, rope 5 m long attached to peg, stick at 5 m mark, keep rope tight, use stick to scratch ground to make circle
18. seventy-five degrees
19. or similar
20. A(0, 3), B(4, 7), C(3, 1)
21. 20 cm, 14 cm
22. 6

English

1. Jianie and Kreen
2. No, Campsie to Kreen is further.
3. south
4. Lake Dyre
5. Jianie to Kreen
6. horizon
7. border
8. b
9. b   10. has
11. are   12. be
13. ox, louse, baby
14. After John recited 'The Man from Snowy River' Mary sang 'Waltzing Matilda'.

Answers

UNIT 12 page 34

Maths

1. 16, 12, 11, 17, 13, 28
2. 5, 8, 9, 6, 7, 29
3. 8, 2, 9, 4, 7, 22
4. one million six hundred and forty-nine thousand and ninety-three
5. 995 147, 1 005 147
6. $\dfrac{29}{50}$
7. $22.90
8. 56%
9. $16
10. no
11. 1200 seconds
12. 4 litres
13. false
14. 15 600
15. cm³
16. true
17. 6 cm
18. 180°
19.
20. south-west
21. 1.9 km
22. June, January

English

1. b
2. d
3. c
4. Great Wall
5. 1c, 2a, 3d, 4b
6. conductor
7. refrigerator
8. a
9. a
10. taller
11. peel
12. worn
13. He struck the match. (or similar)
14. 'Whispering Springs' is a homestead on the banks of the Darling River.

UNIT 13 page 36

Maths

1. 3, 10, 5, 4, 9, 50
2. 1, 4, 2, 7, 3, 49
3. 4, 0, 14, 6, 10, 36
4. 1 659 609
5. neither
6. $\dfrac{15}{24}$
7. $71.55
8. 80%
9. 0.1
10. 18 L
11. 210 minutes
12. 3
13. 182 mm
14. false
15. 51 m³
16. SM −14°C, AS 35°C, S 20°C
17.

    Centre   Diameter   Radius   Circumference
18. 275°
19. none
20. westerly
21. 240 km
22.

Carrots, Tomatoes, Potatoes, Beans

English

1. d
2. d
3. c
4. Latin
5. 1c, 2d, 3b, 4a
6. address
7. biscuit
8. a
9. b
10. load
11. pull
12. damaged
13. He will stand beside the door.
14. I read an interesting story about Elvis Presley in Mum's 'Woman's Day' magazine.

UNIT 14 page 38

Maths

1. 10, 13, 11, 14, 12, 21
2. 7, 9, 1, 8, 3, 90
3. 6, 7, 5, 1, 2, 99
4. 2 000 000 + 500 000 + 80 000 + 3000 + 200 + 60 + 4
5. 1 000 549
6.
7. $3456.85
8. $\dfrac{94}{100} = 0.94 = 94\%$
9. 3 600 000
10. 51
11. $3\dfrac{1}{2}$ hours
12. 6.22 kg
13. A
14. 1 ha
15. 1 m³
16. decreases
17. twice
18. reflex
19. (triangle diagram)
20. south-west
21. a
22. $\dfrac{1}{6}$

English

1. b
2. b or d
3. c
4. dotted
5. d
6. Desert
7. February
8. c
9. c
10. annoyed
11. There
12. these
13. The lion will not go to the spring because he will easily be seen as the moon is shining. (or similar)
14. Near the entrance to the cave Jenna found Dutch, English and Spanish coins.

Answers

Maths

1. 9, 12, 10, 13, 11, 42
2. 7, 9, 6, 1, 8, 79
3. 24, 20, 36, 28, 32, 56
4. 1 074 037
5. 990 000
6.
7. $253.96
8. 26 cents
9. 36.5 mm
10. 1.5 kg
11. ahead
12. 7.256
13. 112 mm
14. more
15. greater
16. 16 °C
17. check drawing
18. 4
19.

20. (4, 2)
21. 5.4 cm
22. 50%, 25%

English

1. a
2. b
3. c
4. wind, fog, clouds
5. c
6. guessed
7. library
8. d
9. c
10. those
11. right
12. here
13. tallest
14. Weren't you at Taronga Park Zoo last Saturday, Meeka?

Maths

1. 16, 13, 11, 14, 11
2. 6, 6, 7, 7, 9, 7
3. 9, 6, 4, 2, 0, 9
4. 4 000 000 + 90 000 + 700 + 10 + 9
5. 995 872, 1 015 872
6.
7. greater by $20.67
8.
9. b
10. 8640 mL
11. 8 hours
12. 500 kg
13. c
14. c
15. b
16. 11 °C
17. a
18. check angle
19.
20. south-east
21. 4 m, 3.5 m
22.

No of eggs

M	◯	◯	◯	
T	◯	◯		
W	◯	◯	◯	◯
T	◯	◖		

◯ = 4 eggs

English

1. b
2. a, b
3. d
4. to calve
5. Project Jonah—Save the Whales
6. calves
7. migrate
8. a
9. d
10. scene
11. forty
12. quiet
13. Because humpbacks are not shy, people can get close to them. (or similar)
14. "Look at the whale doing a back somersault," said the man. "Yes, I have it on film," replied the cameraman.

Maths

1. 8, 11, 13, 17, 15, 26
2. 9, 3, 2, 4, 0, 79
3. 1, 9, 7, 0, 8, 12
4. twenty-nine million three hundred and eighty-six thousand five hundred and ninety-four
5. 13 659 185
6. $\frac{17}{19}$
7. $27.80
8. 0.6 = 60%
9. 3 000 000
10. 4.85 kg
11. 1932 hours
12. 7.058 t
13. millimetres
14. 18 m²
15. 36
16. 37.7°C
17.
18. perpendicular
19. 1, 3, 8, 0
20. (4, 3)
21. 0.5 km
22. Jan and Kath or Jo and Katy

English

1. New South Wales
2. false (he was appointed once then elected four times)
3. <u>Despite the fact that he didn't go to school much as a child, he became a well-respected citizen.</u>
4. From <u>1946</u> to <u>1960</u> he lived on an island near Townsville.
5. c, b, d, a
6. Parliament, independent
7. labourer, Valley
8. given
9. unsuccessful
10. Board
11. practise
12. dairy
13. (a) <u>E</u>lectronic <u>F</u>unds Transfer at <u>P</u>oint <u>O</u>f <u>S</u>ale
    (b) <u>D</u>igital <u>V</u>ersatile <u>D</u>isc
    (c) <u>U</u>niversal <u>S</u>erial <u>B</u>us
    (d) <u>Q</u>ueensland <u>A</u>nd <u>N</u>orthern <u>T</u>erritory <u>A</u>erial <u>S</u>ervices
14. There's now a suburb, an electorate and a <u>U</u>niversity <u>S</u>cholarship named after him.

ANSWERS: *Excel* Basic Skills English and Mathematics Year 6

Answers

UNIT **17** page 48

Maths

1. 12, 10, 16, 13, 7, 17
2. 5, 1, 7, 2, 9, 59
3. 0, 0, 0, 0, 0, 0
4. 71 018 004
5. even
6. twenty-one twenty-fifths
7. $4.90
8. $\dfrac{35}{100} = 35\%$
9. 40
10. 288
11. 2:56 pm
12. 80 t
13. metres
14. 49 m^2
15. 96 cm^3
16. 450°
17. false
18.
19.
20. false
21. 10 cm
22. 100 km

English

1. a and c
2. c
3. a
4. monkeys
5. 1d, 2b, 3a, 4c
6. necessary
7. argument
8. b
9. a
10. fell
11. break
12. male
13. You lent me a book. I am returning it.
14. On 25 March Sir John Cobb left Canberra by Qantas jet for Darwin.

UNIT **18** page 50

Maths

1. 4, 2, 5, 3, 11, 51
2. 1, 4, 0, 3, 9, 74
3. 3, 5, 2, 4, 1, 11
4. 30 000 000
5. 2
6. 0.625
7. $6.39
8. 300 mL
9. $\dfrac{1}{2}$ million
10. 20 L
11. 6 hours 47 mins
12. 12.5 t
13. 637 mm
14. 60 cm^2
15. 58 mL
16. 2.1°C
17. true
18. 180°
19. circle
20. 125 km
21. 1 cm
22. 2 out of 6

English

1. 8:29 am
2. 8:40 am
3. Marcie Road
4. no
5. (a) 9:01 am
   (b) 9:07 am
   (c) 9:14 am
6. burglar
7. possession
8. a
9. b
10. buries
11. seen
12. run
13. This is Mr Brown who lives next door.
14. That's my dog with its tail up in the air.

UNIT **19** page 52

Maths

1. 5, 7, 0, 8, 1, 17
2. 1, 8, 0, 4, 6, 80
3. 7, 6, 4, 0, 1, 26
4. 800 000
5. one
6. 81.79
7. 75 cents
8. 500 g
9. $\dfrac{1}{2}$
10. 60%
11. 0810 or 2010 hours
12. $7\dfrac{1}{2}$ t
13. 3240
14. 12 m^2
15. 324
16. 25 – 35°C
17. 4 sides, 4 angles
18. 50°
19. equilateral
20. A(1, 2), B(4, 4), C(2, 0)
21. 40 times
22.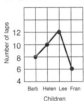

English

1. d
2. a
3. b
4. over 1 million
5. d
6. laziness
7. government
8. c
9. d
10. given
11. steak
12. bear
13. Ingrid is a country girl.
14. "They're making the men's lunches," said Julie Brown.

Answers

UNIT 20 page 54

Maths

1. 10, 6, 3, 7, 12, 51
2. 7, 0, 2, 6, 1, 98
3. 5, 9, 0, 7, 1, 11
4. 5
5. 79 595, 79 600
6. 63.53
7. $3.85 to the nearest 5c
8. 0.55
9. 7 kg
10. $1985.50
11. 23:35
12. 1000
13. yes
14. 9 m²
15. 1000
16. [ruler diagram]
17. [parallelogram diagram] 18. 100°
19. square
20. [grid diagram] 21. 1 : 100
22. 50%, $\frac{1}{4}$

English

1. a
2. c
3. d
4. 180 km
5. c
6. machinery
7. altogether
8. a
9. a
10. fair
11. week
12. come
13. The people standing on the wharf saw a submarine.
14. Isn't that lady's hat very much like yours?

UNIT 21 page 56

Maths

1. 11, 6, 15, 12, 9, 22
2. 8, 4, 0, 5, 9, 13
3. 42, 56, 49, 35, 14, 84
4. A
5. 206 534
6. a
7. same
8. 44%
9. 8 m
10. 660 g
11. behind
12. 31 000 kg
13. 56.347 m
14. 8 m²
15. 38 mL
16. – 5°
17. equal and parallel
18. 30° 19. none
20. north-east 21. 1 : 100
22. [line graph with axes Kilometres (0–500) and Litres (11–66)]

English

1. Tomato paste and tomato sauce.
2. When it has cooked for the required time and before serving.
3. They won't cook if the oil is cold.
4. It makes it easy to see what is needed for the recipe before starting.
5. 10 minutes, as total cooking time is 30 mins
6. believe 7. choose
8. a 9. c
10. lie 11. Lay
12. lie 13. Here
14. Along the border our army was in action. Fresh troops were transported in. A fierce battle was being fought.

UNIT 22 page 58

Maths

1. 15, 18, 12, 9, 14, 68
2. 8, 7, 9, 5, 6, 29
3. 6, 5, 9, 4, 8, 11
4. 28 534 174
5. false
6. a
7. $15.84
8. 0.7
9. $200 – $40 = $160
10. 2989.2 km
11. 3:47 pm
12. 21.35 t
13. same
14. 16 m²
15. 200 mL
16. 260°
17. has only three sides
18. 30°
19. 2
20. south-east
21. 5 m × 2.6 m
22. 20, approximately 30 (27)

English

1. d
2. c
3. c
4. He had heard rumours.
5. c
6. diamonds
7. farther
8. a
9. c
10. spoken
11. farther
12. heard
13. The king's crown was solid gold.
14. Mr Smith and his son, John, will visit Magnetic Island on the Great Barrier Reef.

Answers

Maths

1. 6, 11, 5, 8, 7, 20
2. 9, 1, 0, 5, 3, 10
3. 9, 45, 72, 27, 0, 99
4. 29 202 022
5. composite
6. 0.882 3529
7. $17.45 (rounded to 5c)
8. 90%
9. $60
10. $60 ($56.55)
11. 2 h 15 min
12. 1000 g, 1000 kg, 1 000 000 g
13. 1000 m, 1 km
14. 17 m²
15. 200 cm³   **16.** 160°
17. equal   **18.** 60°
19. true   **20.** north
21. 5 m   **22.** 15

English

1. Albert had little training in art but had much natural talent.
2. 57 years old when he died
3. trees
4. He produced over 2000 paintings.
5. Melbourne
6. great Australian
7. always, real
8. ground-up earth
9. (a) **g**nome (b) lam**b**
   (c) fol**k** (d) cu**p**board
10. His paintings were hung in a gallery.
11. He was finally laid to rest in Alice Springs.
12. It's too expensive to buy.
13. (a) birth
    (b) decrease
    (c) dishonour
    (d) dull (colours)
14. Rex asked, "Do you think you'll become a famous artist with your unique style?"

Maths

1. 3, 6, 8, 12, 15, 19
2. 25, 22, 17, 13, 7, 6, 6
3. 16, 24, 32, 12, 8, 16, 0, 4, 28
4. b
5. 768 760, 788 760, 798 760
6. 0.944 4444
7. $10.15
8. $65 = \dfrac{65}{100} = 0.65 = 65\%$
9. 7 L
10. 3×10L, 2×4L, 1×1L
    (or 4×10 L if you are prepared to waste 1L)
11. 0835 hours
12. cow, dog
13. 8600 cm, 86 000 mm
14. false
15. 2000 mL
16. 114°C
17. true
18. 80°
19. infinite, one
20. (0, 0)
21. check drawing,
    9.7 cm × 4.5 cm
22.

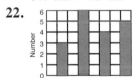

Total 18 stamps

English

1. b   **2.** b
3. d
4. CFCs in washing powder
5. because if one shop doesn't have environmentally safe products, another might
6. manufacturer
7. ingredients
8. d   **9.** a
10. check   **11.** learn
12. labels
13. I saw the advertisement. (or similar)
14. "Safe? Of course our products are safe. Just ask us and we'll tell you," said the salesman.

Answers

UNIT **24** page 66

Maths

1. 4, 5, 7, 9, 11, 41
2. 2, 4, 8, 6, 10, 69
3. 6, 9, 0, 1, 7, 11
4. four million, three hundred and eighty-nine thousand, and ninety-six
5. 0, 2, 4, 6, 8, 10, 12, 14
6. $\frac{6}{10} = 0.6 = 60\%$
7. $27.97
8. $\frac{3}{4}$
9. 600 000
10. 6 × 4 legged, 8 × 3 legged
11. 2 min 42.94 sec
12. a and c
13. 77 mm
14. 10 000
15. 180 m³
16. 80–100 °C
17. parallelogram
18. check angle drawn
19. 4   20.
21. 6.8 m
22. A 1450 km, B 1100 km, C 1400 km

English

1. a   2. a
3. b
4. Queensland and Northern Territory Aerial Service
5. 3a, 1b, 4c, 2d
6. your   7. There's
8. a   9. a
10. does   11. done
12. written
13. I saw him. (or similar)
14. Prince Philip, Duke of Edinburgh, gave an address to the University of Sydney.

UNIT **25** page 68

Maths

1. 7, 8, 6, 2, 1, 90
2. 1, 4, 0, 7, 9, 69
3. 0, 30, 35, 40, 5, 75
4. 1 750 000
5. 161, 163, 165, 167, 169, 171, 173, 175, 177, 179
6. $\frac{1}{5} = 0.2 = 20\%$
7. giant 2.5 kg
8. 70%
9. 7 L
10. $1212
11. 59.85 sec
12. 5460
13. millimetres
14. 173 448 m² = 17.3448 ha
15. 125 m³
16. 75°
17. cone
18. 140°
19. circle
20. east
21. check drawing, 3 cm × 15 mm
22. 7 in 100

English

1. b
2. a
3. c
4. 26 000
5. b
6. unconscious
7. to, irrigate
8. b
9. d
10. ring
11. taught
12. lay
13. The boy with red hair runs fast.
14. "Haven't you seen this little girl's book anywhere?" asked Miss Black.

UNIT **26** page 70

Maths

1. 10, 17, 11, 15, 12, 96
2. 0, 9, 3, 6, 5, 39
3. 4, 6, 1, 7, 0, 11
4. 1 119 572
5. 2, 3, 5, 7, 11
6.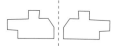
7. $78 profit
8. $\frac{76}{100} = 0.76 = 76\%$
9. 6 t
10. 1.078 t
11. 04:13:56
12. 325 g
13. 17 cm
14. 256 m²
15. 1 kg, 1000 cm³
16. 0–10 °C
17. false
18. degree
19.
20. (0, 5)
21. 25 m × 45 m
22. A(1, 2), B(2, 3), C(3, 2), D(4, 4), E(5, 5), F(6, 3), G(7, 1)

English

1. d
2. b
3. c
4. 5
5. b
6. programme or program
7. skilful
8. b
9. c
10. came
11. saw   12. their
13. axes, oases, sons-in-law
14. "Why," asked Sarah, "did you take Harry's brother to Pelican Creek?"

Answers

Maths

1. 4, 10, 5, 11, 8, 82
2. 7, 3, 9, 6, 8, 89
3. 36, 12, 0, 24, 48, 72
4. 800 000
5. 6, 8, 9, 12
6. $\dfrac{2}{6}$
7. $201.60
8. $\dfrac{63}{100} = 0.63$
9. $3.20
10. $35 550
11. 4:12.63
12. 5 t 30 kg
13. 5 cm
14. 6 m^2
15. 7.015 L
16. 0–25 °C
17. sphere
18. 360°
19. check drawing
20. (4, 0)
21. 450 mm, 45 cm
22.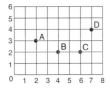

English

1. a, b, d   2. b
3. b   4. c
5. c   6. height
7. though
8. b
9. d
10. written
11. piece
12. scene
13. The boy on the bicycle did not notice the broken window.
14. "The dog," said Sam, "always waits for me outside Woolworths."

Maths

1. 11, 7, 12, 6, 4, 51
2. 6, 7, 0, 4, 9, 40
3. 6, 8, 5, 7, 9, 19
4. 2
5. 288 564, 298 564, 308 564
6. $\dfrac{3}{4}$
7. $13 514
8. seventy-four point five per cent
9. $51.94 to nearest cent
10. 1.74 g
11. 07:40 am, 0740 hours
12. $380
13. 48 cm
14. 40 ha
15. 87
16. 14°
17.
18. 120°
19.
20. (1, 2), (4, 0), (3, 5)
21. 10 mm
22. false

English

1. b
2. c
3. b
4. recently graduated
5. d
6. whistle
7. boundary
8. c
9. c
10. Bow
11. flower
12. too
13. I will write this. (or similar)
14. "Fire!" shouted the captain to his soldiers.

Maths

1. 16, 14, 13, 15, 10, 24
2. 3, 7, 9, 1, 5, 47
3. 56, 0, 48, 32, 24, 80
4. 9
5. 250 000, 200 000, 150 000
6. $\dfrac{15}{24} = \dfrac{20}{32}$
7. $10 296
8. 65%
9. 75 684 000
10. $5.40
11. 1.6 sec
12. 13.288 t
13. square
14. 149 cm^2
15. 16 cm^3
16. 3 °C
17. parallel
18. 53°
19. equilateral
20. north-west
21. check drawing
22.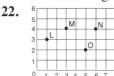

English

1. 15 minutes   2. soaked
3. eight (or seven if hot and boiling water is counted as one ingredient)
4. 1.025 L
5. 1d, 2b, 3a, 4c
6. exercise
7. umbrella
8. a
9. a
10. rowed
11. fair
12. know
13. In the west the storm clouds gathered.
14. "It's gone," whispered Tom. "Let's look for it together," replied Mum.

ANSWERS: *Excel* Basic Skills English and Mathematics Year 6

Answers

UNIT **30** page 78

Maths

1. 6, 2, 7, 1, 10, 95
2. 7, 8, 1, 0, 4, 21
3. 8, 6, 9, 1, 7, 11
4. 2 000 000 + 800 000 + 30 000 + 7000 + 500 + 80 + 4
5. 959 900
6. denominator
7. $4.68
8. $\dfrac{3}{10}$
9. 780
10. 12.214 t
11. 6 min 11.5 sec
12. 20.9 t
13. 26 cm
14. 41 cm²
15. 1.075 L
16.   17. 4
18. 338°
19.
20. (4, 1)
21. 8 km
22. not likely

English

1. c   2. d
3. c
4. letter from promoter
5. a and c
6. valuable
7. pineapple
8. c
9. b
10. raze
11. pane
12. boarder
13. Here is the girl. You wished to see her.
14. "It's a shame that Polly, the parrot, has injured its wing," said Nerellie.

TEST **4** page 80

Maths

1. $12, 16 kg, 8 L, 12 t, 12 cm³
2. 9 kg, 6 kg, 7 kg, 0 L, 3 L, 6 L
3. 18, 24, 48, 60, 30
4. 9
5. 9.9, 10.9
6. 0.875
7. $53.50
8. 12 spaces red, 2 blue
9. correct
10. $13.75
11. 800 m
12. dog, crab
13. rectangle 3 cm × 1 cm
14. 36 cm²
15. completely fill
16. ice
17. true
18. acute, obtuse, straight, reflex, rotation
19.
20. (7, 4), (4, 7)
21. 1 : 5
22. slim

TEST **4** page 82

English

1. a
2. c
3. b
4. emergents
5. 1c, 2d, 3b, 4a
6. rainforest, teeming
7. member, amphibians
8. c
9. b
10. tallest
11. metres
12. it's
13. Giant kapok trees have feathery seeds which are dispersed by the wind. (or similar)
14. "Many creatures (spiders, insects, birds, reptiles, mammals and amphibians) are to be found in the rainforest canopy," our teacher told us.

12. A water tank holds 350 L. If the tank itself has a mass of 150 kg, what is the total mass of a full tank of water?

13. Which of the following ways will not give you the perimeter of a rectangular 2D shape?

(a) find the sum of all the sides   (b) L + B + L + B

(c) 2 × L + B   (d) 2 × (L + B)

(e) double length + double breadth

14. Area means: (Cross out the wrong ones.)

(a) the distance around the edge   (b) the cubic capacity of the shape

(c) the space enclosed within a 2D shape

15. Which of these volume measurements are incorrect?

(a) 15 m³   (b) 38 square centimetres   (c) 561 cubic millimetres

16. The temperature range for Jindabyne was 14˚. If the minimum was –3 ˚C, what was the maximum?

17. Which circle is the largest?

(a) one with a radius of 2.8 cm   (b) one with a diameter of 2.8 cm

(c) one with a circumference of 2.8 cm

18. Use your protractor to draw an angle of 138˚.

19. Use the line of symmetry given to create a symmetrical shape.

20. If ↖ represents North then → represents [   ].

21. On the plan of our new house (scale 1 : 250),
this is the size of my bedroom
What will the real dimensions be?  long

and wide

Statistics and Probability

22. Draw this information on a pictograph.

Mr Finn's hens laid these eggs over 4 days.

Day	No. of eggs	Day	No. of eggs
Monday	12		
Tuesday	8		
Wednesday	16		
Thursday	6		

KEY [ ] =

Whales return

In winter, singing humpback whales can be seen along Australia's east coast. This is the time of their annual migration from the Antarctic seas to warmer waters.

The whales are huge, but very gentle and playful. They make a rumbling, singing sound underwater.

The year 1986 was a good year for the scientists who count the whales. They found that whale numbers had increased greatly.

The humpback whale has been in danger of extinction. Between 1952 and 1963 whalers worldwide had killed more than 7000. In 1963 there were only about 200 of these whales left in the Antarctic.

Killing the Antarctic humpback whale was banned 25 years ago. The whale population has grown fast. Scientists think there may be 700 whales now.

Every four years, scientists go to North Stradbroke Island on the Queensland coast to do a whale count. About forty people (including volunteers) spend ten weeks watching and counting. They watch from Point Lookout, and they use light planes and small boats, as well.

The humpback whale is not shy of humans. People are able to move close, watch their movements, and take photographs. A photographer took a picture of a lively 40-tonne female doing a back somersault above the water.

In winter, southern right whales come to the waters of South Australia. They shelter in quiet bays for the birth of their calves. They are often seen as close as 200 metres from the coast. People watch from the cliffs and the huge sand dunes of the Nullabor Plain. Scientists watch and count the whales from aircraft and from the shore. More than one hundred whales have been seen along these coasts.

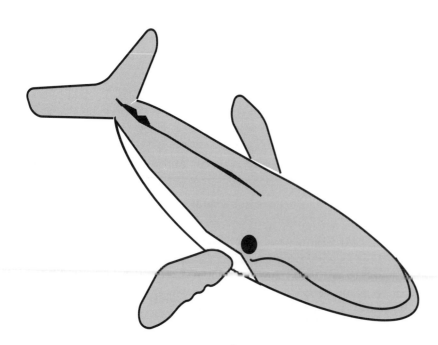

Project Jonah—the save the whale campaign—has been active for many years. Thousands of people, including children, have written letters, made speeches and marched. In some countries, whaling is still allowed, so the campaign goes on.

From *Saving Wildlife* by Edel Wignell

Reading and Comprehension

1. By 1963 how many humpback whales did scientists estimate were left?
(a) 7000
(b) 200
(c) 700
(d) 1952–1963

2. Humpback whales can be seen
(a) in Antarctica.
(b) along the east coast of Australia.
(c) only off the Queensland coast.
(d) from the Nullabor Plain.

3. Humpback whales may be described as
(a) huge.
(b) gentle.
(c) playful.
(d) good singers.
Which one doesn't apply?

4. For what reason do southern right whales visit the coast of South Australia?

_____

_____

5. The last few words state ... _so the campaign goes on_. What campaign?

_____

_____

Spelling and Vocabulary

Rewrite the misspelt words.

6. Whales and their calfs shelter in the quiet bays.

_____

7. Each year the whales migrat along the east coast of Australia.

_____

Circle the word that has the nearest meaning to the underlined word.

8. The <u>campaign</u> has been successful.
(a) organised action
(b) alcoholic drink
(c) people
(d) whale watching

9. Once the humpback was nearly <u>extinct</u>.
(a) plentiful
(b) common
(c) large
(d) died out

Circle the correct word in brackets.

10. The sight of whales is a beautiful (seen, scene).

11. About (forty, fourty) whale watchers gather each year.

12. Whales prefer (quite, quiet) places.

Grammar and Punctuation

13. Join these two sentences without using the word _and_.

The humpbacks are not shy. People can get close to them.

_____

_____

14. Punctuate and capitalise these sentences.

look at the whale doing a back somersault said the man

yes i have it on film replied the cameraman

_____

_____

_____

_____

Mathematics

Number and Algebra

1.

+	0	3	5	9	7	18
8						

2.

−	11	5	4	6	2	81
2						

3.

÷	8	72	56	0	64	96
8						

4. Write 29 386 594 in words.

5. What is the next odd number after 13 659 183?

6. Write seventeen nineteenths in digits.

7. 4 books at $6.95 each will cost $

8. $\frac{3}{5} = 0.$ ☐ = ☐ %

9. Round off 2 756 321 to the nearest million.

10. From a 10 kg bag of rice, 3.2 kg, 900 g, 550 g and $\frac{1}{2}$ kg were used. How much remains?

Measurement and Geometry

11. Write 7:32 pm in 24-hour time.

12. Write 7 tonnes 58 kg in decimal form.

13. What's the best unit of length to measure the thickness of a desk top?

14. 6 m / 3 m — What is the area?

15. How many cubic centimetres would fill a prism 6 cm long, 2 cm wide and 3 cm high?

16. What is the temperature shown on this thermometer?

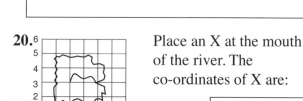

17. Complete this shape to form a parallelogram.

18. Lines which intersect at right angles are ☐ to each other.

19. Write the digits which are symmetrical.

20. Place an X at the mouth of the river. The co-ordinates of X are:

21. On a map the scale of 1 : 10 000 is shown. If the distance between A and B is 5 cm, then the real distance is:

Statistics and Probability

22.

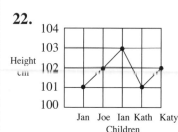

This line graph shows the height of five children. Name two with the same height.

Neville Bonner

Neville Thomas Bonner (28 March 1922 – 5 February 1999) was born at Franklin Island on the Tweed River in northern New South Wales. He had almost no formal education.

He worked as a farm labourer before settling on Palm Island, near Townsville, Queensland, in 1946.

In 1960 he moved to Ipswich, where he joined the board of directors of the One People of Australia League (OPAL), an Indigenous rights organisation. He became its Queensland president in 1970.

He joined the Liberal Party in 1967 and held local office in the party.

In 1971 he was appointed by the Queensland Parliament to represent Queensland in the Senate, thus becoming the first Indigenous Australian to sit in the Australian Parliament. He was elected to the parliament in his own right in 1972, 1974, 1975 and 1980.

While in the Senate he served on a number of committees. However, he disagreed with the Liberal Party on some issues and was dropped from the Liberal Senate ticket in 1983. He then stood as an independent candidate and was nearly successful.

After that he was:

- appointed to the board of directors of the ABC (Australian Broadcasting Corporation)
- named Australian of the Year in 1979
- appointed an Officer of the Order of Australia (OA) in 1984
- a member of the Griffith University Council from 1992 to 1996
- awarded an honorary doctorate in 1993.

He died at Ipswich, aged 76.

Reading and Comprehension

1. In which state was Neville Bonner born?

_____

2. Bonner was elected to parliament five times.

True or false? _____

3. Underline the only statement which is correct.

(a) Despite the fact that he didn't go to school much as a child, he became a well-respected citizen.

(b) He was elected as an Independent candidate in the 1983 election.

(c) A football grandstand in Ipswich is named after him.

(d) The suburb of Bonner in Brisbane bears his name.

4. From _____ (year) to _____ (year) he lived on an island near Townsville.

5. Arrange these statements in the correct order.

(a) He was awarded the Order of Australia.

(b) He became a member of the Liberal Party.

(c) He moved to Ipswich to live.

(d) He was elected President of OPAL.

Spelling and Vocabulary

Rewrite the misspelt words.

6. Neville stood for Parlament as an independant candidate.

7. He worked as a farm laborer in the Tweed Valey.

Circle the word that has the nearest meaning to the underlined word.

8. In 1993 he was <u>awarded</u> an Honorary Doctorate.

(a) studied   (b) earned   (c) given   (d) wrote

Circle the word that means the opposite of the underlined word.

9. He was not <u>successful</u> in that election.

(a) dissuccessful   (b) insucessful

(c) ensuccessful   (d) unsuccessful

Circle the correct word in brackets.

10. He served on the (Bored, Board) of Directors of the ABC.

11. At no time did he (practice, practise) as a lawyer.

12. I saw him when he visited our local (diary, dairy).

Grammar and Punctuation

13. OA is an abbreviation for Order of Australia. For what do these abbreviations stand?

(a) EFTPOS _____

(b) DVD _____

(c) USB _____

(d) QANTAS _____

14. Punctuate and capitalise this sentence.

theres now a suburb an electorate and a university scholarship named after him

_____

_____

Number and Algebra

1.

+	5	3	9	6	0	10
7						

2.

–	12	8	14	9	16	66
7						

3.

×	5	6	8	7	1	99
0						

4. Write in digits: seventy-one million and eighteen thousand and four.

5. Is 76 583 122 odd or even?

6. Write $\frac{21}{25}$ in words.

7.

$ 10 – [85 c 85 c 85 c / 85 c 85 c 85 c] =

8. $\frac{7}{20} = \frac{}{100} = \boxed{}$ %

9. 28 564 172 + 11 302 516 =

approximately [ ] million

10. There were two children for every adult attending the concert. 864 tickets were sold. How many adults were at the concert?

Measurement and Geometry

11. Write 14:56 in am/pm time.

12. An adult blue whale could weigh 80 g, 80 kg or 80 t?

13. Which unit would I use to measure the distance from the school gate to the classroom?

14. Find the area.
7 m
7 m

15. Find the volume.
3 cm
4 cm
8 cm

16. What is the temperature shown on this thermometer?
400° 500°
300° 600°

17. This shape is a parallelogram. True or false?

18. Draw a line segment which is perpendicular to this line.

19. Draw a rectangle and show its lines of symmetry.

20. On a grid (1, 5) and (5, 1) are the same point. True or false?

21. I have a 1 : 40 scale model of a car. The real car is 4 m long. How long is my model?

Statistics and Probability

22. Megan graphed the distance she would travel at 40 km/h.

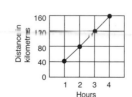

How far would she travel in $2\frac{1}{2}$ hours?

Rainforests

Logging and clearing for settlement and agriculture are the main causes for the destruction of rainforests. Around the world increasing populations mean that the rainforest is under threat as people clear it for settlement. Every year large sections of the Amazon rainforest are burnt in order to clear land for grazing and for cash crops. In Africa and South-East Asia, logging for sawn timber, plywood and woodchips for paper is being carried on at rates that are not sustainable. Logging also opens up forests to other influences. Settlers move in. Hunters use logging roads to gain access to the forest. Hunters often have a destructive effect on the forest. When they kill and capture the largest and most spectacular animals, they remove not only the animals but also the important ecological functions the animals perform. For instance, monkeys in South-East Asia are important in releasing the seeds of the rambutan tree from the fruit. Removing the monkeys endangers the rambutan tree and everything that depends on it.

From *Rainforests* by Stephen Jones

Reading and Comprehension

1. Amazonian rainforests are cleared for
   (a) grazing.   (b) settlement.
   (c) crops.   (d) all of these reasons.

2. The major threat to rainforests comes from
   (a) hunters.   (b) loggers.
   (c) increased population.   (d) animals.

3. Most of the trees cleared in the Amazon are
   (a) burnt.
   (b) logged for sawn timber.
   (c) made into plywood.
   (d) chipped for paper.

4. Name the animal responsible for the dispersal of rambutan seeds.

   _____

   _____

5. Number the statements in order (1–4).
   (a) Roads give access to the forest.
   (b) Rainforest is cleared for land.
   (c) Hunters go into the forest.
   (d) Population increases.

Spelling and Vocabulary

Rewrite the misspelt words.

6. It's not neccessary for you to do that.

   _____

7. Don't get into an arguement
   over things like that. _____

Circle the word that has the nearest meaning to the underlined word.

8. Mr. Smith's knowledge of horology is extensive.
   (a) horror stories   (b) clocks
   (c) astrology   (d) horses

9. The Kon Tiki was built from balsa.
   (a) light wood   (b) steel
   (c) reeds   (d) drums tied together

Circle the correct word in brackets.

10. Timbergetters (fell, fall) trees in the forest.

11. The cup did not (brake, break) when it fell.

12. A (mail, male) duck is a drake.

Grammar and Punctuation

13. Divide this sentence into two smaller sentences.

    I am returning the book that you lent me.

    _____

    _____

14. Punctuate and capitalise this sentence.

    on 25 march sir john cobb left canberra by qantas jet for darwin

    _____

    _____

Number and Algebra

1.

+	2	0	3	1	9	49
2						

2.

–	4	7	3	6	12	77
3						

3.

÷	18	30	12	24	6	66
6						

4. Round off 26 513 021 to the nearest ten million.

5. The first prime number is:

6. Convert $\frac{5}{8}$ to a decimal.

7.  What will 3 loaves of bread and 2 tubs of margarine cost?

8. Find 30% of 1 litre.

9. Is 547 968 closer to $\frac{1}{2}$ million or 600 000?

10. Of the contents of a drum, 55% or 11 litres remain. How much would the drum hold?

Measurement and Geometry

11. How long does it take us to get to the coast if we leave home at 7:28 am and get there at 2:15 pm?   hrs   mins

12. Write 12 500 kg in tonnes.

13. Write 63.7 cm in mm.

14. 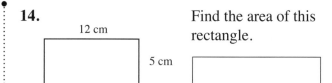 Find the area of this rectangle.

15. A shape holds 58 cm³ of water. What volume of water is this?

16. My temperature is 39.1 °C. How high above normal is this?

17. A rectangle is a special parallelogram. True or false?

18. In a triangle the total of the three angles is:

19. Which shape has the greatest number of lines of symmetry?

20. 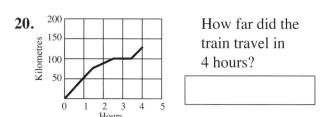 How far did the train travel in 4 hours?

21. A microscope magnifies things 100 times. An ant appears to be 1 metre long, but it is really only   long.

Statistics and Probability

22. 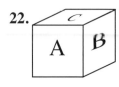 This die has the first six letters of the alphabet on it. What are the chances of rolling a vowel?

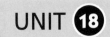
Reading timetables

Buses travelling to the school each morning

Narrington Street Depot

| 7:45 | 7:58 | 8:15 | 8:29 | 8:40 | 8:52 |

Marcie Road

| 7:48 | 8:01 | 8:18 | 8:32 | 8:43 | 8:55 |

Lighton Road

| 7:52 | 8:05 | 8:22 | 8:36 | 8:47 | 8:59 |

Jewel Street

| 7:54 | 8:07 | 8:24 | 8:38 | 8:49 | 9:01 |

Arch Avenue

| 7:57 | 8:10 | 8:27 | 8:41 | 8:52 | 9:04 |

Trench Road

| 8:00 | 8:13 | 8:30 | 8:44 | 8:55 | 9:07 |

Shearer Road

| 8:03 | 8:16 | 8:33 | 8:47 | 8:58 | 9:10 |

Carlyle Street

| 8:05 | 8:18 | 8:35 | 8:49 | 9:01 | 9:12 |

Den Place

| 8:07 | 8:20 | 8:37 | 8:51 | 9:04 | 9:14 |

School

| 8:09 | 8:22 | 8:39 | 8:53 | 9:07 | 9:16 |

Reading and Comprehension

1. What would be the most suitable bus to catch from the depot for a 9 am start at school?

_____

2. Margaret lives at Arch Avenue and wants to catch the same bus. What time should she be at the bus stop?

_____

3. When the 7:58 bus is at Carlyle Street where is the 8:15 bus?

_____

4. Has the 8:29 bus left the Narrington Street Depot before the 7:58 reaches the school?

_____

5. What time does the 8:52 am reach
(a) Jewel Street? _____
(b) Trench Road? _____
(c) Den Place? _____

Spelling and Vocabulary

Rewrite the misspelt words.

6. The dog attacked the burgular. _____

7. Cook took posession of the east coast of Australia in 1770. _____

Circle the word that has the nearest meaning to the underlined word.

8. The farmer wore his <u>brogues</u> into town.
(a) shoes   (b) glasses
(c) work clothes (d) best shirt

9. Put these events into <u>chronological</u> order.
(a) order of importance (b) order of time
(c) order of size   (d) order of logic

Circle the correct word in brackets.

10. Fido (buries, berries) his bones.

11. Have you (saw, seen) him?

12. I must (run, ran) or I'll be late.

Grammar and Punctuation

13. Join these sentences by using *who*, *whom* or *whose*.

This is Mr Brown. He lives next door.

_____

_____

14. Punctuate and capitalise this sentence.

thats my dog with its tail up in the air

_____

_____

Number and Algebra

1.

+	5	7	0	8	1	17
0						

2.

–	9	16	8	12	14	88
8						

3.

×	7	6	4	0	1	26
1						

4. What is the value of the 8 in 23 812 657?

5. One (1) cannot be prime as it has only [ ] factor.

6. Write eighty-one point seven nine in digits.

7. 4 cans for $3 — What is the cost of one can?

8. What's 25% of 2 kg?

9. $49\frac{1}{2}\%$ is very nearly equal to $\frac{1}{2}$, 0.55 or $\frac{56}{100}$?

10. I've completed 0.4 of my project. What % remains to be done?

Measurement and Geometry

11. in 24-hour time is: [ ]
(Two answers are possible.)

12. Write seven and a half tonnes in shortened form.

13. There are [ ] millimetres in 3.24 m.

14. 6 m / 2 m — What is the area of this floor?

15. 324 mL of water will fill a volume of [ ] cm^3.

16. Circle the approximate temperature range for an average summer's day.
$0 – 5°C, 5 – 15°C, 15 – 25°C, 25 – 35°C$

17. A parallelogram must have [ ] sides and [ ] angles.

18. 50° / x — What is the size of $\angle x$?

19. Name the triangle which has 3 lines of symmetry.

20.

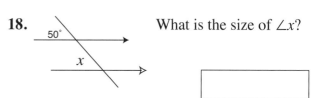

Name the co-ordinates of:
A
B
C

21. An overhead projector image of a 5 cm long pencil is 2 m. How many times has the image been magnified?

Statistics and Probability

22. Draw a line graph to show the laps children completed in a Jog-a-thon.

Children	Barb	Helen	Lee	Fran
No. of laps	8	10	12	6

Number of laps

Children

Made for Australia

One afternoon in 1952, Sydney inventor Mervyn Victor Richardson was working in his backyard workshop in the suburb of Concord. He joined a petrol engine to a rotary mower (its blades turned in a circle for cutting) and so caused a revolution in lawnmower design. The new Victa could be easily adjusted to cut different kinds of grass: high or low, tough or soft. It was ideal both for mowing a beautiful lawn and for hacking away at the rough stuff. You never had to sharpen the blades or trim round trees in the old backbreaking way, because the Victa was able to cut right up to walls, paths, trees and garden borders.

By 1956 over 60 000 of his Victa rotary lawnmowers were being made each year. Today, well over one million Victa machines have been produced using the original rotary principle.

From Made for Australia by Judith Kendra

Reading and Comprehension

1. Which conditions of grass are Victa mowers suitable for?
   (a) high or low
   (b) tall, tough grass
   (c) short, soft grass
   (d) high or low, tough or soft

2. The blades of a Victa turn in a
   (a) horizontal plane.
   (b) vertical plane.
   (c) inclined plane.
   (d) revolutionary plane.

3. The name Victa comes from
   (a) the word 'victor' (it defeats grass).
   (b) the inventor's name.
   (c) the manufacturer's name.
   (d) the name of Richardson's workshop.

4. How many Victa mowers have been produced?

   _____

5. Which of the following is not an advantage of Victa mowers?
   (a) Blades never need sharpening.
   (b) They can be used on any type of grass.
   (c) They have height adjustment.
   (d) They can be made in a backyard workshop.

Spelling and Vocabulary

Rewrite the misspelt words.

6. Your lazyness will not help you to win.

   _____

7. The goverment cannot help all people all the time.

   _____

Circle the word that has the nearest meaning to the underlined word.

8. Meet me in the <u>foyer</u>.
   (a) doorway   (b) entrance
   (c) hallway   (d) main room

9. The group will <u>ostracise</u> him for his behaviour.
   (a) applaud   (b) praise
   (c) not forget   (d) exclude

Circle the correct word in brackets.

10. I have (gave, given) him the answer.

11. May bought a kilogram of (stake, steak).

12. I can't (bear, bare) it any more.

Grammar and Punctuation

13. Rewrite this sentence using one word for the underlined phrase.

    Ingrid is a girl <u>from the country.</u>

    _____

14. Punctuate and capitalise this sentence.

    theyre making the mens lunches said julie brown

    _____

    _____

Number and Algebra

1.

+	7	3	0	4	9	48
3						

2.

−	7	0	2	6	1	98
0						

3.

÷	20	36	0	28	4	44
4						

4. Which digit is in the millions column in 25 386 272?

5. Continue these multiples of 5.

79 585, 79 590, ____, ____

6. Which is greater, 63.53 or sixty-three point three five?

7. 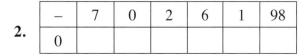 $0.87   95c   What change will I get from $20 after buying 6 pads and a dozen pens?

8. Which is greater, 0.55 or 50%?

9. Round off 7 kg 97 g to the nearest kg.

10. What will I pay for a computer priced at $2090 if I get a 5% discount for cash?

Measurement and Geometry

11. in 24-hour time is: ____ pm

12. There are ____ kg in 1 tonne.

13. Bill is 1356 mm tall. Is this possible?

14. Calculate the area of this square in m².

300 cm

300 cm

15. A litre of water fills ____ cm³.

16. Show −8 °C on this thermometer.

0°   10°

17. Complete this parallelogram.

18. What is the size of ∠y?

80° y

19. Which has more lines of symmetry, a rectangle or square?

20.

4
3
2
1
0 1 2 3 4

Put a circle around the grid reference (0, 0)

21. An object was drawn to scale firstly as 1 : 10, and then as 1 : 100. Which would be the smaller drawing?

Statistics and Probability

22. This pie graph shows food sold at a canteen.

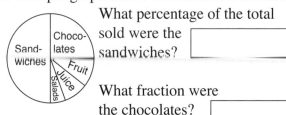

Sand-wiches   Choco-lates   Fruit   Juice   Salads

What percentage of the total sold were the sandwiches?

What fraction were the chocolates?

Antarctica

One of the great challenges was to reach the South Pole. Because Antarctica is a continent, this involved making a long journey from a coastal base across land covered in ice and snow. Ernest Shackleton made an attempt in 1908–09 and was forced to turn back 180 kilometres from the Pole. In 1911–12 a race for the South Pole developed between two separate expeditions: a British one led by Captain Robert Falcon Scott; and a Norwegian one led by Captain Roald Amundsen.

Scott's party (five men for the final stage of the trip) reached the South Pole on 18 January 1912, only to find a tent and the Norwegian flag flying. Amundsen had got there first (on 14 December 1911). This disappointment for Scott was followed by tragedy, for his party did not get back to their base alive. Their bodies (and their diaries) were found the next summer by other members of their expedition.

From *Antarctica* by John Collerson

Reading and Comprehension

1. Which of the following best describes Antarctica?
   (a) a frozen continent
   (b) a large landmass of snow
   (c) an island covered in ice
   (d) one of the continents of the world

2. The first attempt to reach the Pole was made by
   (a) Scott.   (b) Amundsen.
   (c) Shackleton.   (d) Scott's party of five.

3. The South Pole was reached
   (a) in 1908–09.
   (b) in 1911–12.
   (c) on 18 January 1912.
   (d) on 14 December 1911.

4. How close did Shackleton get to the Pole?

   _____

5. Which of these statements is implied, but not stated?
   (a) Amundsen reached the Pole first.
   (b) Scott's party did not come back alive.
   (c) Amundsen survived the journey.
   (d) Scott and four others perished in Antarctica.

Spelling and Vocabulary

Rewrite the misspelt words.

6. Keep away from dangerous mashinery.

   _____

7. Alltogether there are five good-sized fish.

   _____

Circle the word that has the nearest meaning to the underlined word.

8. I'll meet you at the tram <u>terminus</u>.
   (a) end stop   (b) stop
   (c) shed   (d) line

9. <u>Vault</u> over this log.
   (a) leap   (b) fall
   (c) climb   (d) straddle

Circle the correct word in brackets.

10. "It's not (fair, fare)," she said.

11. I'll be here for a (weak, week).

12. Hasn't the mailman (come, came) yet?

Grammar and Punctuation

13. Reorganise this sentence so that it makes sense.

    The people saw a submarine standing on the wharf.

    _____

    _____

14. Punctuate and capitalise this sentence.

    isnt that ladys hat very much like yours

    _____

    _____

Number and Algebra

1.

+	5	0	9	6	3	16
6						

2.

–	16	12	8	13	17	21
8						

3.

×	6	8	7	5	2	12
7						

4. Which 4 has the greater value in 14 382 415, A or B?
    A   B

5. Which number comes next?

236 534, 226 534, 216 534,

6. $6.9 + 3.21$ should be set out:
Circle your choice.

(a) $\begin{array}{r} 6.9 \\ +\ 3.21 \\ \hline \end{array}$ (b) $\begin{array}{r} 6.9 \\ +\ 3.21 \\ \hline \end{array}$

7. Which is greater,
50% of \$5 or $\frac{1}{4}$ of \$10?

8. Circle the greatest fraction.

$\frac{4}{10}$,   0.4,   44%,   4%

9. Is 8 m 7 cm closer to 8 m or 9 m?

10. A can has a mass of 60 g. Half full the can weighs 360 g. What will a full can weigh?

Measurement and Geometry

11. Darwin is 1 hour (ahead of / behind) Sydney.

12. Write 31 t in kilograms.

13. Write 56 347 millimetres in metres.

14. Find the area of a rectangle 4 m long and 200 cm wide.

15. I have an irregular shaped object with a volume of 38 cm³. What volume of water will this equal?

16. Which is closer to 0 °C, –5 °C or –9 °C?

17. Opposite sides of a parallelogram are [ ] and [ ].

18.  ∠z is equal to:

19. Show the lines of symmetry on this parallelogram.

20. If ↖ represents North then ↑ is [ ].

21. A 5 m tall tree appears to be 5 cm tall in a photograph. What is the scale of the photograph?

Statistics and Probability

22. Draw this information on a line graph.

Litres	11	22	33	44	55
Kilometres	100	200	300	400	500

Kilometres

Litres

Delicious Spaghetti Bolognaise

Ingredients:
1/2 packet spaghetti
2 tablespoons oil
1 kg minced meat
2 finely chopped onions
1/2 bottle tomato sauce
250 g bottle tomato paste
Salt and pepper to taste

Method:
1. Cook the spaghetti in boiling water.
2. Heat oil in another pot.
3. Add meat and chopped onion and cook for twenty minutes.
4. Stir in the tomato paste, sauce, salt and pepper.
5. Leave to simmer.
6. Strain the spaghetti and serve with the sauce.

(Cooking time 30 minutes.)

Reading and Comprehension

1. Name the two items made from tomatoes in this recipe.

_____

2. When do you strain the spaghetti?

_____

3. Why are the meat and onions placed in heated oil and not cold?

_____

_____

4. Why is the recipe written with the list of ingredients and then the method?

_____

_____

5. If the meat and onion cook for twenty minutes, how long will the tomato paste and sauce need to simmer?

_____

Spelling and Vocabulary

Rewrite the misspelt words.

6. I do not beleive you.

_____

7. Chose which one you'd like to have.

_____

Circle the word that has the nearest meaning to the underlined word.

8. Mary is <u>bilingual</u>.
    (a) speaks two languages
    (b) lingers around places
    (c) pays for guests
    (d) very intelligent person

9. Flinders was the first European to <u>circumnavigate</u> Australia.
    (a) find   (b) explore
    (c) sail around   (d) name

Circle the correct word in brackets.

10. I like to (lie, lay) in the shade.

11. (Lie, Lay) the book on the table.

12. Don't tell me a (lie, lay).

Grammar and Punctuation

13. Rewrite the underlined group of words as one word.

<u>In this place</u> we shall build a city.

_____

14. Punctuate and capitalise this text.

along the border our army was in action fresh troops were transported in a fierce battle was being fought

_____

_____

_____

_____

Number and Algebra

1.

+	6	9	3	0	5	59
9						

2.

–	13	12	14	10	11	34
5						

3.

÷	36	30	54	24	48	66
6						

4. Add a million to 27 534 174.

5. There are more odd numbers less than 50 than even numbers. True or false?

6. 84.1 – 7.92 must be set out as: Circle your choice.

  (a) 84.1
     – 7.92

  (b) 84.1
     – 7.92

7. | Legs of Pork | 3.2 kg will cost:
  | $4.95 / kg |

8. I was offered 0.7 or 7% of a chocolate cake. Which is the larger share?

9. $197.46   is approximately $
     – 38.97   –

10. Dad's truck uses 3 L of petrol every 10.6 km. The fuel tank holds 846 L. How far can he go without refuelling?

Measurement and Geometry

11. It takes $4\frac{1}{2}$ hours to travel to our grandmother's home. We leave at 11:17 am. What time will we arrive?

12. An empty truck has a mass of 5.1 t. Loaded it weighs 26.45 t. What is the mass of the load?

13. Which is longer; 1 m, 100 cm or 1000 mm?

14.  Find the total area of these shapes.

15. What is the volume of the object?

16. What is the temperature shown here?

17. Give a reason why this shape is not a parallelogram.

18. How big is ∠a?

19. A rhombus has 0, 2 or 4 lines of symmetry?

20. What direction is found at 135° clockwise from North?

21. 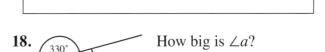 This is a scale drawing of a room. If the scale is 1 : 200, then the real dimensions are:

Statistics and Probability

22. What is the difference between the greatest and the least number of cars?

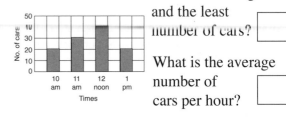

What is the average number of cars per hour?

Indonesia

Nearly 1000 years ago, in 1006, a devastating earthquake shook western Java. The volcano Merapi erupted at the same time, smothering everything for kilometres around with lava, ash and landslides. In terror, the people fled as far as they could. Those who could not escape died in the fury of the volcano.

And so it was that ancient Borobodur was forgotten for more than 800 years. The world's largest Buddhist monument, built a little more than a century before the volcano erupted, lay undisturbed below layers of lava and ash, smothered by dense jungle.

The ruins were not rediscovered until 1814. Indonesia was under temporary British rule at the time, and the Lieutenant-Governor, Sir Thomas Stamford Raffles (who later founded Singapore), had heard rumours about ancient sculptures in the area near Magelang. He sent one of his engineers, HCC Cornelius, to explore the area. Imagine the astonishment of the search party when the huge hill they were standing on turned out to be the top of a massive stone monument.

From *Indonesia* by Lisa Hill

Reading and Comprehension

1. Borobodur was built
   (a) 800 years ago.
   (b) in 1006.
   (c) a thousand years ago.
   (d) before 1006.

2. Borobodur was rediscovered by
   (a) Sir Thomas Stamford Raffles.
   (b) Magelang.
   (c) HCC Cornelius.
   (d) the Indonesian Buddhists.

3. The monument was covered by
   (a) an earthquake.   (b) landslides.
   (c) lava and ash.   (d) a volcano.

4. What made Raffles send Cornelius looking for the monument?

_____

5. Which of these statements logically follow on from the passage?
   (a) The area was left alone as there could be more eruptions.
   (b) The sculptures were found and taken away to museums.
   (c) The area was carefully excavated and restored to the best possible condition, considering the damage from the volcano.
   (d) The area was carefully excavated and restored to its original glory.

Spelling and Vocabulary

Rewrite the misspelt words.

6. Dimonds are a girl's best friend.

_____

7. This is father than I thought it would be.

_____

Circle the word that has the nearest meaning to the underlined word.

8. He gave my paper a <u>cursory</u> glance.
   (a) quick   (b) thorough
   (c) curt   (d) slow

9. Do you understand the <u>gravity</u> of this situation?
   (a) pull   (b) size   (c) importance   (d) need

Circle the correct word in brackets.

10. She has always (spoke, spoken) the truth.

11. Is it much (father, farther)?

12. I (herd, heard) the sound of gunfire.

Grammar and Punctuation

13. Rewrite the sentence using one word for the underlined phrase.

    The crown <u>belonging to the king</u> was solid gold.

    _____

14. Punctuate and capitalise this sentence.

    mr smith and his son john will visit magnetic island on the great barrier reef

    _____

Number and Algebra

1.

+	1	6	0	3	2	15
5						

2.

−	16	8	7	12	10	17
7						

3.

×	1	5	8	3	0	11
9						

4. What number is one million less than 30 202 022?

5. All even numbers (except 2) are also c __ __ p __ __ __ __ __ __ numbers.

6. Use your calculator to convert $\frac{15}{17}$ to a decimal.

7. $3\frac{1}{2}$ kg of lamb at $4.99/kg is:

8. 0.9 = 9% or 90% or 99%?

9. 29 articles at $1.95 would cost approximately:

10. Calculate the exact cost of the articles in Question 9.

Measurement and Geometry

11. What is the difference between 2:15 pm and 1630 hours?

12. There are ____ g in a kg. There are ____ kg in a tonne, so there must be ____ g in a tonne.

13. I walked 1 000 000 millimetres, or ____ m or ____ km.

14.  Find the area of the shaded part of this shape.

15. What is the cubic capacity of the object?

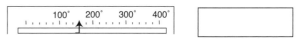

16. What temperature is shown here?

100° 200° 300° 400°

17. A rhombus is a special parallelogram. All sides are ____ in length.

18. 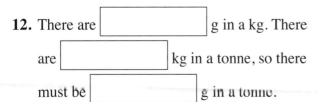 How big is the unnamed angle?

60°
60°

19. Naturally occurring objects are seldom perfectly symmetrical. True or false?

20. Name the direction 360° from North.

21. This circle has been drawn to a scale of 1 : 500. What is the radius of the real circle?

Statistics and Probability

22. This graph shows the number of buses that left a bus station between 1 pm and 3 pm on 3 days.

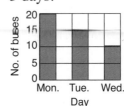

What is the average for the three days?

Albert Namatjira

Elea Namatjira was born on 28 July 1902 and raised at the Hermannsburg Mission in the Northern Territory. His parents changed his name to Albert after he was baptised. At the age of 13, Namatjira was initiated and became a member of the Arrernte community. When he was 18 he married his wife Rubina. In his early life he worked as a camel driver and saw much of Central Australia, which he later used as the main subject of his paintings.

In 1936 Namatjira acted as a guide for the artist Rex Battarbee, and showed him the local area. In return Albert was shown how to paint with watercolours, a skill at which he quickly excelled.

Namatjira developed a unique style of painting which highlighted the rugged features of the outback in the background, with the distinctive Australian majestic white gum trees surrounded by twisted scrub in the foreground. Namatjira loved painting trees. The colours he used in his landscapes were similar to the ochres that his ancestors used.

In 1938 his first exhibition was held in Melbourne. For 10 years Namatjira continued to paint. His paintings sold quickly because of his rising popularity and he became quite wealthy but he was always glad to return to the outback.

By the time of his death Namatjira had painted a total of nearly 2000 paintings. Even today Namatjira's work is still on display in some of Australia's major art galleries.

Albert Namatjira, one of the greatest Australian artists and pioneer for Aboriginal rights, died of heart disease complicated by pneumonia on 8 August 1959 in Alice Springs.

Reading and Comprehension

1. In your opinion which of these statements is true?
   (a) Albert was taught how to paint by Rex Battarbee.
   (b) Albert was a self-taught artist.
   (c) Albert had little training in art but had much natural talent.
   (d) Albert studied his art through art galleries and art colleges.

2. Albert Namitjira was
   a) 56 years old when he died.
   b) 57 years old when he died.
   c) 34 years old.
   d) 59 years old.

3. What was his favourite subject to paint?
   (a) trees   (b) flowers
   (c) ochre   (d) camels

4. Cross out the statement that is not true about Albert.
   (a) He produced over 2000 paintings.
   (b) He developed his own unique style of painting.
   (c) Albert only became an artist later in his life.
   (d) He did not marry Rubina before 28 July 1920.

5. When and where was the first public display of his art?

   _____

Spelling and Vocabulary

Rewrite the misspelt words.

6. He was a grate Australia artist.

7. His watercolours allways looked so reel.

8. Which phrase has the same or nearly the same meaning as the underlined word?
   The colours were similar to ochre.
   (a) bright red and blue colours
   (b) those made from charcoal
   (c) ground-up earth
   (d) those used by all artists

9. The word *pneumonia* begins with a silent letter. Circle the silent letters in these words.
   (a) gnome   (b) lamb   (c) folk   (d) cupboard

Circle the correct word in brackets.

10. His paintings were hung in a (galley/gallery).

11. He was finally (lain/laid) to rest in Alice Springs.

12. (It's/its) (to/too/two) expensive to (by/bye/buy).

Grammar and Punctuation

13. Write the opposite of the following words.
    (a) death   _____
    (b) increase   _____
    (c) honour   _____
    (d) bright (colours) _____

14. Punctuate and capitalise this sentence.

    rex asked do you think youll become a famous artist with your unique style

    _____

    _____

Mathematics

Number and Algebra

1. Name all the landing points on this number line.

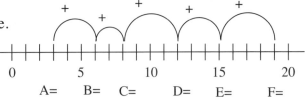

A=   B=   C=   D=   E=   F=

2. I started with 27, took 2 ⬚ , subtracted 3 ⬚ , then found 5 less ⬚ ,

   minus 4 ⬚ , found the number 6 fewer ⬚ , and then subtracted 1 ⬚ .

   I am now left at number ⬚ .

3. Multiply each of the numbers round the circle by the number in the centre. Write your answers outside the circle.

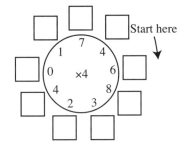

4. Which 8 has the greater value, A or B?   785 842   68 087 828
                                                    A   B

   ⬚

5. Complete: 758 760 , ⬚ , 778 760 , ⬚ , ⬚

6. Use your calculator to change $\frac{17}{18}$ to a decimal.

   ⬚

7. I buy a tracksuit for $59.95, a basketball for $29.95 and a pair of shoes for $49.95. What is the change from three $50 notes?

   ⬚

8. $\frac{13}{20}$ = ⬚ hundredths = $\frac{⬚}{100}$ = 0.⬚ = ⬚ %

9. Is 7 litres 87 millilitres closer to 7 L or 8 L?

   ⬚

10. 1 litre of paint costs $19.95, 4 litres $38.90 and 10 litres $73.50. What is the cheapest way to purchase 39 litres?

    ⬚

Measurement and Geometry

11. My analogue clock reads 25 to 9 in the morning. My digital watch reads 8:35 am. What would a 24-hour clock read?

    ⬚

12. Cross out the ones which would not be measured in tonnes.
    cow, truck, ship, elephant, dog

    ⬚

13. 86 metres = [_____] cm = [_____] millimetres

14.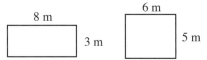

These two rectangles have the same perimeter. They also have the same area. True or false? [_____]

15. A piece of stone in the shape of a cube raises the water in a measuring cylinder by 2000 mL. The volume of the added stone is:

16. What is the difference between 340 °C and 226 °C?

17. A rectangle is a special parallelogram.
What makes it special is that it has 4 equal angles. True or false? [_____]

18.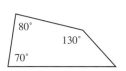

Without using your protractor, what is the size of the fourth angle?

19. A circle has [_____] lines of symmetry, but a semicircle has only [____] line of symmetry.

20.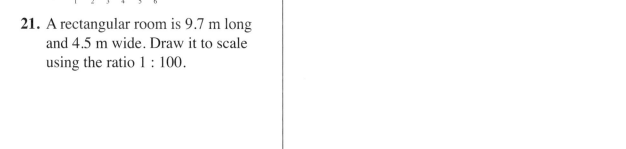

Name the co-ordinates of the point that is 3 spaces SW of the position X. [_____]

21. A rectangular room is 9.7 m long and 4.5 m wide. Draw it to scale using the ratio 1 : 100.

Statistics and Probability

22. Draw on a column graph the types of stamps a boy has collected.

Origin of stamp	USA	Fiji	Brazil	France
Number	3	6	4	5

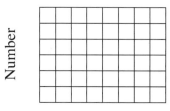

Number

Countries

How many stamps are there altogether? [_____]

How to become a careful consumer

Environmentally friendly products are becoming more and more popular. It is in the economic interest of companies to follow this trend. Many manufacturers have become increasingly careful about the items they produce and the ways in which they advertise. Unfortunately there are some companies that are taking advantage of this trend, claiming that their products are 'environmentally safe' when in fact they are not. One company proudly claims that its washing powder does not contain CFCs—CFCs have never been used in washing powders!

Many companies are designing labels around an environmental theme (such as an animal or a picturesque outdoor scene). This strategy does not ensure, however, that the product is 'safe'. You should still check the ingredients on the label. Many countries are preparing to establish guidelines ensuring that products claiming to be 'environmentally safe' are really that.

Becoming an environmentally aware consumer requires more time when you shop. You should:

- select products carefully—never shop on an empty stomach and always have a shopping list prepared

- read labels to find out what ingredients are contained in products and if they are harmful

- visit several shops to find what you want.

It seems an effort but it is worth taking the time, knowing that you are helping to save the planet.

When you go shopping select items that:

- are energy efficient
- can be recycled/reused
- are safe to your health
- are not over-packaged.

From *Earth First* by Jenny Dibley & David Bowden

Reading and Comprehension

1. What is meant by *in the economic interest of companies*?
(a) Companies work for the economy.
(b) It's good business for the company.
(c) The company is interested in economics.
(d) If they don't do it they'll go out of business.

2. In buying environmentally-safe items you should
(a) check the label for pictures.
(b) check the label for the ingredients.
(c) try it out.
(d) ask the storekeeper.

3. It is stated that you should *never shop on an empty stomach*. This means
(a) you'll get hungry and eat food in the shop without paying.
(b) you'll rush to get home to eat.
(c) you'll make poor choices because you're hungry.
(d) you could be tempted to buy more (especially food) than you really need.

4. Give an example of misleading advertising.

_____

_____

5. Why should you visit several shops before purchasing?

_____

_____

_____

Spelling and Vocabulary

Rewrite the misspelt words.

6. He's a manufacturerer of soap powder.

_____

7. Check the ingreedients on the label.

_____

Circle the word that has the nearest meaning to the underlined word.

8. You need to be a responsible <u>consumer</u>.
(a) person
(b) adult
(c) child
(d) user

9. The <u>ingredients</u> need to be checked.
(a) what is in it
(b) what is not in it
(c) poisons
(d) natural items in it

Circle the correct word in brackets.

10. (Check, Cheque) out the advertisement.

11. We need to (teach, learn) how to save the planet.

12. Read (labels, lapels) to find out the ingredients.

Grammar and Punctuation

13. "Manufacturers advertise their products."

Here *advertise* is a verb. Use the noun form of this word in a sentence.

_____

_____

_____

_____

14. Punctuate and capitalise this text.

safe of course our products are safe just ask us and we'll tell you said the salesman

_____

_____

_____

Number and Algebra

1.

+	2	3	5	7	9	39
2						

2.

−	8	10	14	12	16	75
6						

3.

÷	54	81	0	9	63	99
9						

4. Write 4 389 096 in words.

5. List the first 8 even numbers.

6. $\dfrac{3}{5} = \dfrac{\boxed{}}{10} = 0.\boxed{} = \boxed{}\%$

7. What is the cost of 3.5 kg of pork at $7.99/kg?

8. Which is greater, 70% or $\dfrac{3}{4}$?

9. Estimate the answer by rounding off.

$$704\ 683$$
$$-\ 129\ 544$$

10. Dan makes 3 and 4 legged stools. He has 14 seats and 48 legs. How many of each type can he make?

Measurement and Geometry

11. What is the difference between 6 min 28.5 sec and 3 min 45.56 sec?

12. Which of the following would you measure in tonnes?
(a) the bricks to build a house
(b) a motor cycle   (c) a train carriage

13. How long is this line segment?   mm

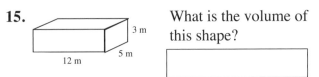

14. There are _____ square metres in a hectare.

15. 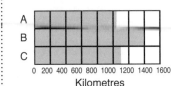 What is the volume of this shape?

16. Circle the approximate temperature range for a cup of tea.
0–20 °C, 20–40 °C, 40–60 °C,
60–80 °C, 80–100 °C

17. Name the 2D shape which has opposite sides equal and opposite sides parallel, but no right angles.

18. Draw an angle of 28°.

19. A square has turn symmetry of _____ .

20. Plot the points A(5, 0), B(3, 2) and C(1, 4).

21. This line segment has been drawn to 1 : 100 scale. The real line is _____ m long.

Statistics and Probability

22. This graph shows the distance 3 people have travelled from Sydney. How far must each travel to reach their destination at 2500 km?

QANTAS

Australians are a most air-minded people, with a network of airways crisscrossing our vast land like the web of a crazy spider.

Born in Queensland on 16 November 1920, the Queensland and Northern Territory Aerial Service consisted of the capital sum of £6037 ($12 074) and two flimsy First World War aircraft—90 hp (horsepower), air-cooled engine RAF two seaters—with a cruising speed of sixty-five miles per hour.

The two men who claimed to be and are indeed the founders of this company were two WW1 veteran pilots who served with the Royal Australian Flying Corps—P J (Ginty) McGinness and Wilmot Hudson Fysh (who was later knighted for his work in developing this airline).

That year the first ticket was issued to a pioneer pastoralist, eighty-seven-year-old Alexander Kennedy of Longreach. His first, and the company's first, flight was a four-hour thirty-five minute flight from Longreach to Cloncurry. It is worth noting that Alexander Kennedy had made the reverse journey fifty-three years previously in a bullock wagon and that journey had taken him eight months.

Today, QANTAS services not only stretch across Australia but to the major cities and continents of the world.

Reading and Comprehension

1. When we changed from pounds (£) to dollars ($), a pound was converted into
    (a) $2.   (b) 50c.   (c) $1.   (d) $5.

2. If a mile equals 1.61 km, then the speed of their first plane was
    (a) 104.65 km/h.   (b) 40.37 km/h.
    (c) 161 km/h.   (d) 65 km/h.

3. When did Alexander Kennedy settle in Longreach?
    (a) 1920   (b) 1867
    (c) 1860   (d) 1833

4. For what do the letters QANTAS stand?

    _____

    _____

5. Link these dates and people with the events.

    (a) McGinness & Fysh   (1) the first QANTAS passenger

    (b) Alexander Kennedy   (2) the first flight took place

    (c) 16 November 1920   (3) served as pilots in WWI

    (d) 1920   (4) QANTAS came into being

Spelling and Vocabulary

Rewrite the misspelt words.

6. You shouldn't do that to youre young sister.

    _____

7. Theres the mistake you made. _____

Circle the word that has the nearest meaning to the underlined word.

8. It was a lethal weapon.
    (a) life-taking   (b) long   (c) effective   (d) large

9. I will not pay their exorbitant fees.
    (a) excessive   (b) expensive
    (c) demanded   (d) enlarged

Circle the correct word in brackets.

10. My friend (does, dose) not look well.

11. She has (did, done) the work.

12. Have you (wrote, written) the letter?

Grammar and Punctuation

13. Write a sentence using *see* in its past form.

    _____

14. Punctuate and capitalise this sentence.

    prince phillip duke of edinburgh gave an address to the university of sydney

    _____

Mathematics

Number and Algebra

1.

+	7	8	6	2	1	90
0						

2.

–	4	7	3	10	12	72
3						

3.

×	0	6	7	8	1	15
5						

4. Write one and three quarter million in digits.

5. Write the odd numbers between 160 and 180.

6. $\dfrac{\boxed{}}{5} = \dfrac{20}{100} = 0.\boxed{} = \boxed{}\%$

7. SUDSO 1.5 kg $2.96   GIANT SUDSO 2.5 kg $4.90   Which is the better buy?

8. $\dfrac{7}{10}$ = 7% or 70%?

9. Is 7.38 L seven or eight litres when rounded off?

10. Mike pays $1397 for the parts for a computer and sells them for $1599. How much profit will he make on the sale of 6 computers?

Measurement and Geometry

11. Which is closer to 1 minute, 59.85 sec or 1:00:37 sec?

12. There are _____ kg in 5.46 tonnes.

13. What unit would you use to measure the thickness of a cupboard door?

14. Use your calculator to find the area of this rectangle.
803 m
216 m

15. Find the volume of this 5 m cube.
5 m

16. What is the temperature shown on this dial?
70° 80° 60° 90°

17. Which 3D shape has a circular base and an apex?

18. Measure this angle.

19. Name the 2D shape which has an infinite number of turn symmetry.

20. If → is North, then ↓ represents _____.

21. Draw a rectangle 3 m long and 150 cm wide to a scale of 1 : 100.

Statistics and Probability

22. There are 100 tickets in a raffle. If I buy 7 tickets for a dollar, what are my chances of winning the prize?

68

Kaibab deer

"Should people interfere with nature?" is an often asked question.

Last century the Kaibab Plateau in Arizona (USA) was estimated to have had a population of about 30 000 deer. The population was controlled by natural methods—the amount of feed, old age and of course, predators, namely coyotes, mountain lions and wolves. Nature was in balance. Between 1889 and 1908 this area not only had deer, coyotes, mountain lions and wolves, but also thousands of sheep and cattle, which had been introduced and were grazing the area. Sheep in particular compete with deer for range forage. The result was obvious. The deer herd numbered only 4000 by 1907, whilst the sheep and cattle numbered 195 000. The predators still had their food supply. From 1907 to 1923 it was decided that the deer needed help. 3000 coyotes, 674 mountain lions and 11 wolves were killed (by 1939 wolves in this area were extinct). You may think that this would have been good for deer numbers. Yes it was! The population soared to around 100 000. But—nature intervened and the population crashed to 40 000 due to starvation in the severe winters of 1924 and 1925—and continued to fall till today where the deer population of this area is about one third of what it was before humans intervened.

Reading and Comprehension

1. Predators are
    (a) large animals.
    (b) animals which prey upon other animals.
    (c) carnivorous animals.
    (d) herbivores.

2. Which of these animals directly compete with deer for food?
    (a) sheep   (b) cattle
    (c) coyotes   (d) mountain lions

3. The current deer population in the area today is
    (a) 30 000.   (b) 40 000.
    (c) 10 000.   (d) 100 000.

4. By 1907 the deer herd had decreased by
    _____.

5. In your opinion the author is in favour of
    (a) increasing deer population.
    (b) leaving nature alone to maintain its balance.
    (c) wiping out all predatory animals.
    (d) reducing the number of sheep and cattle in this area.

Spelling and Vocabulary

Rewrite the misspelt words.

6. Hang was found unconsious on the ground.

    _____

7. The doctor told the nurse too irigte the wound.

    _____

Circle the word that has the nearest meaning to the underlined word.

8. They gazed at the dromedary.
    (a) two-humped camel (b) one-humped camel
    (c) young camel   (d) Arabian camel

9. Because of the flood the family was destitute.
    (a) saved   (b) separated
    (c) needed new clothing   (d) in great need

Circle the correct word in brackets.

10. Did she (ring, rang) the bell?

11. My father (taught, learned) me how to swim.

12. Will you (lie, lay) the table?

Grammar and Punctuation

13. Rewrite this sentence using a group of words for the underlined phrase.

    The red-haired boy runs fast.

    _____

14. Punctuate and capitalise this sentence.

    havent you seen this little girls book anywhere asked miss black

    _____

    _____

Number and Algebra

1.

+	2	9	3	7	4	88
8						

2.

–	1	10	4	7	6	40
1						

3.

÷	32	48	8	56	0	88
8						

4. Which number is a quarter of a million more than 869 572?

5. List the first six prime numbers.

6. Show $\frac{7}{8}$ on this model.

7. Buying price $850. Selling price $928. Profit / Loss is:

8. $\frac{19}{25} = \frac{\boxed{}}{100} = 0.\boxed{} = \boxed{}\%$

9. Round 5538 kg to the nearest tonne.

10. From a tank holding 1.54 t of fuel oil, 30% is used. How much remains?

Measurement and Geometry

11. Show four minutes thirteen point five six seconds on this digital stopwatch.
$\_\_ : \_\_ . \_\_$

12. 1 dozen cans Spaghetti. Total 5.2 kg. Mass of carton 256 g. Mass of 1 can 87 g. What is the mass of spaghetti in each can?

13. 107 mm or 17 cm. Which is the greater length?

14. What is the area of a square with a side of 16 m?
16 m², 64 m or 256 m²

15. One litre of water has a mass of ☐ kg and a volume of ☐ cm³.

16. Circle the approximate temperature range for a refrigerator.
0–10 °C, 10–20 °C, 20–30 °C, 30–40 °C

17. A 2D shape has length, breadth and height. True or false?

18. The unit used to measure angles is called a:

19. Draw the reflection of this shape.

20.  Name the co-ordinate which is 3 spaces north-west of A.

21. This is the scale drawing of a paddock, using the scale 1 : 1000. What are the real dimensions?

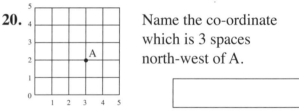

Statistics and Probability

22. Name the co-ordinates.

A(,)	B(,)
C(,)	D(,)
E(,)	F(,)
G(,)	

26 Fletcher Parade
North Kinsbridge NSW 2068

The Manager   24 July 1997
ABC Concrete
Sanuel St
North Kinsbridge

Dear Sir

Our recently formed cricket team, the North Kinsbridge Warriors, have been raising funds to build a new pitch on our new oval in Main Street. So far we have raised enough money to pay for the excavation and the necessary steel reinforcing, but it appears our fundraising will fall short of our target despite the efforts of all of our team. The season will commence on 28 August—only a few weeks away, and we have yet to raise the funds for the concrete.

Mr Ryan, our coach, believes we have a good chance this season, especially on a new wicket (the old one we hoped to use had to be pulled up as it was badly cracked). At our last team meeting, I was elected to write to you seeking your support for our team. We all know how much you support sport in our district.

Any help you can provide will be greatly appreciated.

I look forward to hearing from you soon.

Yours faithfully

Jimmy Carson (V. Captain)

Reading and Comprehension

1. Which item isn't needed for the pitch?
   (a) steel mesh   (b) concrete
   (c) excavation   (d) labour

2. Why was the old pitch pulled up?
   (a) It was too old.
   (b) The surface had become uneven.
   (c) It was too short.
   (d) The positioning was incorrect.

3. Why doesn't the club have the money to pay for the pitch?
   (a) The team wasn't working hard enough.
   (b) They only needed to pay for half of the work.
   (c) The team worked but didn't reach their goal.
   (d) Mr Ryan needed them for practice.

4. How long is it (in weeks) until the season commences?

5. Which of these statements are implied but not stated?
   (a) Mr Ryan manages ABC Concrete.
   (b) The team hopes the manager of ABC Concrete will donate the necessary concrete.
   (c) The Warriors will win the premiership.
   (d) The manager of ABC Concrete follows junior cricket.

Spelling and Vocabulary

Rewrite the misspelt words.

6. The programm is now full. _____

7. Tina is very skillfull in playing the piano. _____

Circle the word that has the nearest meaning to the underlined word.

8. The fox eluded the hounds.
   (a) fooled   (b) escaped from
   (c) outsmarted   (d) ran away

9. The acoustics in the Opera House are outstanding.
   (a) furnishings   (b) sound effects
   (c) sound properties (d) audiences

Circle the correct word in brackets.

10. My neighbour (came, come) home later.

11. I (saw, seen) them this morning.

12. Here they built (their, there) homes.

Grammar and Punctuation

13. Write the plurals of the following words.

   axis _____ oasis _____

   son-in-law _____

14. Punctuate and capitalise this sentence.

   why asked sarah did you take harrys brother to pelican creek

   _____

   _____

Number and Algebra

1.

+	1	7	2	8	5	79
3						

2.

−	16	12	18	15	17	98
9						

3.

×	6	2	0	4	8	12
6						

4. What is the value of the 8 in 2 835 724?

5. Fill in the missing composite numbers.

4, ___ , ___ , ___ , 10, ___

6. If $\frac{1}{6}$ is red and $\frac{3}{6}$ blue, what part is unshaded?

7. Balance $186.20. Deposit $14.55. Interest $3.55. Bank charges $2.70 New balance =

8. $\dfrac{\boxed{}}{100} = 0.\boxed{} = 63\%$

9. 35.6c × 9 = $ ___

10. A property is 237 000 m². If it sells for $1500 per hectare, what is the selling price?

Measurement and Geometry

11. Mimi missed the start of the race by 0.89 sec. Her watch recorded 4:13.52 when she finished. What should the reading have been?

12. Write 5.03 tonnes in tonnes and kilograms.

13. Measure this line to the nearest cm.

14. 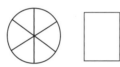 What is the area of the shaded part?

4 m, 3 m

15. Write 7 L 15 mL in decimal form.

16. Circle the approximate temperature range of a piece of cheese.

0–25 °C, 25–50 °C, 50–75 °C, 75–100 °C

17. Name the 3D shape which is totally symmetrical.

18. A full rotation measures ___ degrees.

19. Slide this shape 8 spaces to the right.

20. Each grid square represents 1 km. From A go 3 km East, then 4 km South. Name the co-ordinates of this point.

21. An overhead projector enlarges objects 18 times. A paper clip 25 mm long will appear to be ___ on the screen.

Statistics and Probability

22. Plot these co-ordinates.
A(2, 3) , B(4, 2) ,
C(6, 2) , D(7, 4)

The First Settlement

Governor Arthur Phillip arrived at Botany Bay on the *Supply* on 18 January 1788. The remaining ten ships of the First Fleet arrived the next day. After examining the site it was decided that Botany Bay was too exposed to winds, too shallow a harbour and not a good site for settlement, though fresh water was no problem. On 22 January Captain Phillip, with Captain Hunter, set out to examine Port Jackson. Within two days they reported that they had found one of the finest harbours in the world, in which a thousand ships might ride in perfect security.

Botany Bay was evacuated and all ships assembled in Port Jackson, where it was decided to make a permanent settlement. At Sydney Cove, land was cleared for an encampment as well as storehouses and other buildings. It was recorded: "In the evening of January 26, 1788, the colours were displayed on shore and the Governor, with several of his principal officers and others assembled round the flagstaff, drank the King's health and to the settlement with all display of which such occasions is esteemed propitious."

This day is now celebrated as Australia Day though some historians would prefer 22 August, as this was when Captain James Cook claimed (in 1770) the east coast of Australia in the name of the King of England.

Reading and Comprehension

1. For which of the following reasons was Botany Bay rejected as a site for settlement?
   (a) harbour not deep enough
   (b) not a good place for a permanent camp
   (c) short of water
   (d) winds blew across the open area

2. How many ships comprised the First Fleet?
   (a) 10　　　　　　　　(b) 11
   (c) less than 10　　　(d) more than 11

3. Which group of people might not celebrate Australia Day?
   (a) historians
   (b) Aboriginals
   (c) descendants of convicts
   (d) sailors

4. Why do you think the first settlers of Australia, the Aboriginals, are not mentioned in this passage?
   (a) There were none living at Botany Bay.
   (b) The author forgot about them.
   (c) The extract is written from a European point of view.
   (d) They weren't sailors, farmers, builders or convicts.

5. The passage in quotation marks is not in the style of language we use. This is because
   (a) it was written by adults.
   (b) it is in the language used by sailors.
   (c) it was recorded 200 years ago.
   (d) Governor Phillip was important so anything written about him must sound important.

Spelling and Vocabulary

Rewrite the misspelt words.

6. What's your correct hieght? _____

7. Through you tried, the opposition was too good. _____

Circle the word that has the nearest meaning to the underlined word.

8. Remove the <u>bung</u> from the cask.
   (a) lid　　(b) stopper　　(c) tap　　(d) lid

9. We stayed in a <u>chalet</u> at Jindabyne.
   (a) motel　　　　　　(b) hotel
   (c) hostel　　　　　(d) Swiss-style cottage

Circle the correct word in brackets.

10. Have you (wrote, written) to Mary?

11. A (peace, piece) of fruit is in the bowl.

12. It's a very pretty (scene, seen).

Grammar and Punctuation

13. Rewrite the sentence so that it makes sense.

   The boy did not notice the broken window on the bicycle.

   _____

14. Punctuate and capitalise this sentence.

   the dog said sam always waits for me outside woolworths

   _____

Number and Algebra

1.

+	7	3	8	2	0	47
4						

2.

–	8	9	2	6	11	42
2						

3.

÷	30	40	25	35	45	95
5						

4. Which digit in 2 076 987 has the greatest value?

5. Count on in 10 000s from 278 564.

6. Which is the greater fraction, $\frac{3}{4}$ or $\frac{2}{3}$?

7. New car price was \$17 549. After 12 months the value has depreciated by \$4035. Current value is:

8. Spell out 74.5%.

9. 76.5 litres of petrol at 67.9c per litre costs \$

10. A box of paper clips (contents 150) has a mass of 289 grams. The box weighs 28 g. What is the mass of each clip? (Use your calculator.)

Measurement and Geometry

11. Show 20 to eight in the morning on these digital faces.

| : | am pm | | 24 hour |

12. Sugar costs 38 cents a kg. What will a tonne cost?

13. Calculate the perimeter.

3 cm   3 cm
3 cm   1 cm
6 cm   40 mm 4 cm 6 cm
        40 mm
14 cm

14. A field is 800 m long and $\frac{1}{2}$ km wide. Find its area in hectares.

15. A stone with a volume of 87 cm³ will raise the water level in a measuring cylinder by [ ] millilitres.

16. In the high country the temperature fell from 9° to minus 5°. What is the difference in temperature?

17. Draw the model of a triangular prism.

18.  What is the size of ∠x?

19. Turn this shape 90° clockwise.

20. Name the vertices of this triangle.

21. A film projector shows the image of a creature 10 m tall. If the projector enlarges 1000 times, then the creature is [ ] mm tall on the film.

Statistics and Probability

22. The odds of winning a prize in Lotto is 1 : 850. This means that if I buy 850 entries I must win a prize. True or false?

Star gazer

Nancy watched her computer screen closely. It was now her turn to search the part of the Milky Way for that Black Hole which her calculations said should be there. Mt Stromlo was a busy observatory and she had to wait her turn like all astronomers, but as she had only recently graduated, she had to wait till last.

The coordinates were entered. The dome slowly revolved and the giant mirror turned in its cradle to face the direction given by the computer. Nancy scanned the area. No Black Hole there. The coordinates must be incorrect. Nancy's attention focused on an object that appeared to be moving. She checked the star charts. It wasn't there. She looked back at the screen. It was not a star, not a planet, not a comet. It was a … She was unsure, but she was sure of one thing—it was moving! More calculations were made. The printer began to hum and then started printing. What she now thought was being confirmed. It was an asteroid. Not distant but close—only 1000 million kilometres away. Its size, 8 km in diameter. Composition, mainly iron.

Her next thoughts were, "From where did it come and to where is it going?" More calculations. While the computer calculated she gazed at the image. She had a hunch, a premonition, something worried her. The data came from the computer. Her worst fears were realized … it would strike the Earth in less than a week. Heaven help us.

Reading and Comprehension

1. Mt Stromlo is
    (a) a radio telescope.
    (b) a reflecting telescope.
    (c) a small telescope.
    (d) the largest in the world.

2. In astronomical terms 1000 million kilometres is
    (a) distant.   (b) very distant.
    (c) not far away at all.   (d) a huge distance.

3. The image on this telescope is first picked up by
    (a) radio waves.
    (b) light reflecting on a mirror.
    (c) a computer.
    (d) a video screen.

4. Which phrase tells you that Nancy was not an experienced astronomer?

    _____

5. In your opinion why was she so worried?
    (a) She had found an asteroid.
    (b) The asteroid may hit the Earth.
    (c) The asteroid was 8 km across.
    (d) An asteroid this size could do great damage when it hit Earth.

Spelling and Vocabulary

Rewrite the misspelt words.

6. Wistle while you work. _____

7. The bondary fence does need some repair.

    _____

Circle the word that has the nearest meaning to the underlined word.

8. The <u>defoliation</u> of the plant was caused by a chemical.
    (a) rapid growth   (b) death
    (c) loss of leaves   (d) changed shape

9. He is a member of the <u>elite</u> team.
    (a) winning   (b) losing
    (c) especially selected (d) mediocre

Circle the correct word in brackets.

10. (Bow, Bough) to your audience.

11. There is a (flower, flour) which eats insects.

12. It's (to, two, too) late now.

Grammar and Punctuation

13. Write a sentence using *write* so that it refers to the future.

    _____

    _____

14. Punctuate and capitalise this sentence.

    fire shouted the captain to his soldiers

    _____

Number and Algebra

1.

+	9	7	6	8	3	17
7						

2.

–	7	11	13	5	9	51
4						

3.

×	7	0	6	4	3	10
8						

4. Which digit in 1 038 729 has the least value?

5. Count backwards from 300 000 in 50 000s.

6. $\dfrac{5}{8} = \dfrac{15}{\boxed{}} = \dfrac{\boxed{}}{32}$

7. Una bought $8500 worth of shares last year. These shares have increased by $1796. What is their current value?

8. Which is the greater fraction, $\dfrac{5}{8}$ or 65%?

9. Give an approximate answer to:
$$\begin{array}{r} 75\ 684 \\ \times\quad 996 \end{array}$$

10. A dozen eggs cost $2.16. What will 30 cost?

Measurement and Geometry

11. Bill ran the race in 4:38.5. Hank did it in 4:36.9. What is the difference in their times?

12. An empty bus has a mass of 9.7 t. The average mass of a passenger is 78 kg. The bus holds 45 passengers. What is the total mass of a full bus, including the driver?

13. Which has the greater perimeter, a square of sides 16 cm or a rectangle 18 cm long and 13 cm wide?

14.  What is the total area of this shape?

15. 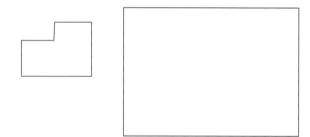 Find the volume.

16. Water from a tap is 19 °C. Water from the fridge is 16° cooler or ___ °C.

17. The sides of a cylinder are ___ .

18. What is the size of $\angle x$?

19. Name the type of triangle which does have turn symmetry.

20. If ↖ is South then → is ___ .

21. Double the size of this shape.

Statistics and Probability

22. Plot these co-ordinates.
L(1,3) , M(3, 4) , N(6, 4) , O(5, 2)

76

How to make bubble bath oil

Ingredients:

250 mL (1 cup) good quality soap or Lux Flakes

1 L (4 cups) boiling water into which 6 sprigs of rosemary or lavender approximately 20 cm long have been steeped for 15 mins.

25 mL (2 tbsp) witch-hazel

50 mL (4 tbsp) glycerine

12.5 mL (1 tbsp) wheatgerm oil

Few drops of lavender oil

25 mL (2 tbsp) of hot tap water

Directions:

1. Dissolve the soap in the rosemary or lavender water.
2. Mix witch-hazel, glycerine, wheatgerm and lavender oils.
3. Pour into a blender with the soap mixture and blend for 5 minutes.
4. Pour into a screw-top bottle and add hot tap water to make a good consistency.
5. Pour a few drops into the bath water.

Reading and Comprehension

1. How long should the rosemary or laven der have been steeped for?

_____

2. What is another word for *steeped*?

_____

3. How many ingredients in total are needed to make bubble bath oil?

_____

4. What is the total amount of water needed?

_____

5. Number these steps in order (1–4).
   (a) Pour into a blender.
   (b) Mix witch-hazel, glycerine, wheatgerm and lavender oils.
   (c) Pour into the bath water.
   (d) Steep the rosemary or lavender.

Spelling and Vocabulary

Rewrite the misspelt words.

6. Exersise is good for your health.

_____

7. The umberella was blown inside out by the gust of wind.

_____

Circle the word that has the nearest meaning to the underlined word.

8. It was a <u>ferocious</u> attack.
   (a) fierce
   (b) sudden
   (c) unprovoked
   (d) unwanted

9. The building was of <u>gargantuan</u> proportions.
   (a) giant   (b) beautiful
   (c) small   (d) intricate

Circle the correct word in brackets.

10. She (rode, road, rowed) across the lake.

11. It's not (fair, fare).

12. I don't (know, no, now) the answer.

Grammar and Punctuation

13. Rewrite this sentence.

    The storm clouds gathered in the west.

    In _____

    _____.

14. Punctuate and capitalise this text.

    its gone whispered tom lets look for it together replied mum

    _____

    _____

    _____

Mathematics

Number and Algebra

1.

+	5	1	6	0	9	94
1						

2.

–	7	8	1	0	4	21
0						

3.

÷	56	42	63	7	49	77
7						

4. Expand 2 837 584.

5. What number is one more than 959 899?

6. To convert a common fraction to a decimal fraction, you divide the numerator by the

.

7. A soft drink costs $1.17 for 1.25 L. What will 5 L cost?

8. Circle the fraction which is incorrect.

$$\frac{3}{5} = \frac{3}{10} = 0.60 = 60\%$$

9. If 9.95% is equal to 78, 100% is approximately:

10. What is the mass of the load on this truck?

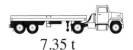

7.35 t   19 564 kg

Measurement and Geometry

11. A machine makes a part in 1:14.3 sec. How long will the machine take to make 5 of these parts?

12. Which is greater, 20.9 t or 20 t 90 kg?

13. A rectangle 7 cm long and 6 cm wide has a perimeter of 13 cm, 42 cm or 26 cm?

14. What is the area of the shaded part of this shape?

9 cm   5 cm   2 cm   2 cm

15. One litre and seventy-five millilitres in decimal form is [ ] L.

16. Show 260 °C on this oven dial.

200°   100°   300°

17. Does a tetrahedron have 2, 4 or 6 sides?

18. Calculate the size of the reflex angle.

22°

19. Draw the line(s) of symmetry in this shape.

20. From (0, 0) go north-east 3 spaces, east 1 space, and south 2 spaces. Name this point.

21. On a map (scale 1 : 250 000) two hills are 3.2 cm apart. Use your calculator to work out the real distance.

Statistics and Probability

22. Certain, good chance, even chance, not likely or impossible? Using one of the terms above, rate the probability of rolling a 7 using 2 dice, three times in a row.

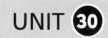
14 Yuledale St
West Morgan 2785
30 June '97

Dear Jake

I had to write to you to let you know the great news.
I was going to ring you but Uncle Ryan said that you
were off travelling and wouldn't be back for a few days.
But the important part—remember that I told you I'd
entered that contest and the first prize was a trip
for a family of four to visit Disneyland for a week—well
guess what? I WON!!

Mum and Dad still don't believe it, but I got a letter
from the promoter of the contest, Mr Cambell, down
in Sydney and it definitely states that I am the winner.
This means we can go as soon as Dad can arrange for
a week's holiday. I'm so excited. It'll be great. The trip
there is by QANTAS from Sydney to Los Angeles, then
transfer to Disneyland. We'll be staying in a hotel just
outside Disneyland and we can go every day for five
whole days, then there's the flight home. I don't think
I'll miss going to school that week very much.

I wish you were coming too but it's only for four and
Connie certainly won't stay home by herself; she's too
young and wants to go as much as I do.

Ring me when you get back and let me know how your
very first job is getting on.

Best wishes
Candice

Reading and Comprehension

1. Jake is Candice's
    (a) uncle.   (b) brother.
    (c) cousin.   (d) aunt.

2. West Morgan is
    (a) an inner suburb of Sydney.
    (b) an outer suburb of Sydney.
    (c) a town in Queensland.
    (d) a town in NSW.

3. When there, their accommodation will be
    (a) in Los Angeles.
    (b) in Disneyland.
    (c) near Disneyland.
    (d) near Los Angeles.

4. What proved to Mum and Dad that she had
won the prize?

_____

5. From your reading of the letter, which feeling(s)
is (are) expressed?
    (a) The writer is very excited about winning.
    (b) Candice is very happy about Connie
        wanting to go.
    (c) Candice would prefer Jake to go instead
        of Connie.
    (d) Candice is a little scared of flying to the USA.

Spelling and Vocabulary

Rewrite the misspelt words.

6. We all learned a valueable lesson today.

_____

7. The pinapple is an introduced, or exotic, fruit.

_____

Circle the word that has the nearest meaning to the
underlined word.

8. Her <u>haughty</u> looks did not impress me.
    (a) good (b) pretty (c) arrogant (d) inappropriate

9. The oil <u>magnate</u> bought two new cars.
    (a) driller   (b) wealthy person (c) buyer (d) seller

Circle the correct word in brackets.

10. The soldiers will (raise, raze, rays) the city.

11. The (pain, pane) of glass broke.

12. Our (border, boarder) pays his rent every week.

Grammar and Punctuation

13. Break up this sentence into two separate ones.

Here is the girl whom you wished to see.

_____

14. Punctuate and capitalise this sentence.

its a shame that polly the parrot injured its
wing said nerellie

_____

Number and Algebra

1.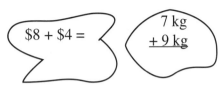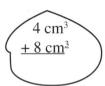

$8 + $4 =

7 kg
+ 9 kg

5 L
+ 3 L

7 t
+ 5 t

4 cm³
+ 8 cm³

2. 15 kg – 6 kg = [   ]   6 L – 6 L = [   ]

15 kg – 9 kg = [   ]   6 L – 3 L = [   ]

15 kg – 8 kg = [   ]   6 L – 0 L = [   ]

3. Circle the numbers which are exactly divisible by 6.

23   38   24   15   48   52

   9   18   19   27   60   30

4. Circle the digit with least value in 27 586 349.

5. Complete this series.   5.9, 6.9, 7.9, 8.9, [   ] , [   ] .

6. $\frac{7}{8}$ = 0.857. Check, and correct if necessary. [   ]

7. Magella bought a bike for $45 and sold it to Pete for a profit of $8.50.

Pete paid [   ] for the bike.

8. On this shape show $\frac{3}{4}$ red and $\frac{1}{8}$ blue.

9. Without calculating, get an approximate idea whether the answer is correct or not. [   ]
98% of 31.5 t = 30.87 t

10. A kilogram of potatoes costs $2.50. What will $5\frac{1}{2}$ kilograms cost? [   ]

Measurement and Geometry

11. A car covers a distance of 100 metres every 7.5 seconds.

In a minute it will have covered [   ] metres.

12. Tick the items you wouldn't measure in tonnes.

13. Draw a rectangle which has a perimeter of
8 centimetres. (The sides are to be in whole centimetres.)

14. 6 cm

6 cm

This square has a perimeter of 24 centimetres.
What is the area?

15. 10 cm
10 cm   10 cm

1 litre of water would (partly fill / completely fill / overflow) this open
cube. Circle the correct answer.

16. Below 0 °C water becomes [   ].

17. A 3D shape is given that name because it has three dimensions;
length, breadth and height/thickness. True or false?

18. Arrange these angles in size from smallest to largest.
Rotation, Obtuse, Straight, Reflex, Acute

19. Redraw this shape, turned 135° clockwise.

20.  If a square is built upon AB, what will the co-ordinates
of the missing points be?

21. The same line is drawn to two scales. The first scale is 1 : 5 and the
second is 1 : 8. Which drawing is longer?

Statistics and Probability

22. I put 3 red, 2 blue and 2 white flowers into a box and shuffle the box.
What is the chance of drawing out, in order, 3 red, then 2 blue, then 2 white?
Good / Likely / Average / Slim / None

Rainforest structure

Despite the diversity in the species in them, tropical rainforests around the world share a number of common features.

The tropical rainforest is a layered environment. When we stand on the floor of a tropical rainforest we find it humid and dark. We also wonder where the bustling life that is supposed to live there is. In fact, most of it is above us in the **canopy**. Just beneath the canopy we have the hall of the forest which is made up of the trunks of trees and under our feet is the forest floor.

The canopy is the powerhouse of the tropical rainforest. It is often divided into three or more layers. Trees reach up forming the canopy, capturing the sun's rays that provide the energy for the whole ecosystem. So thickly do the leaves crowd that as little as one per cent of the light that falls on the canopy reaches the forest floor. Insects, spiders, centipedes, mammals, reptiles, amphibians and birds teem in the canopy 15 to 40 metres above the ground. Half of the Earth's animals live in this environment.

While the top of the canopy is exposed to full sunlight and the wind, within and below the canopy it is darker, more humid and protected.

Towering above the canopy are the **emergents**—the tallest trees in the tropical rainforest. The environment around the crowns of these trees is quite different to that of the canopy. It is windier, less humid and sunnier. They do not host the masses of epiphytes that live in the canopy. Their seeds, like the feathery seeds of the giant kapok, are dispersed by the wind. Often they are the perches for eagles which hunt for food in the canopy. It is not only the plant life that is layered. So too is animal life. Many animals live in only one layer of the rainforest.

The floor of the rainforest is remarkably easy to walk through. With so little light penetrating the canopy there is little vegetation at ground level. It is only where a giant tree has fallen and broken the canopy, or along a road or river, that it becomes impenetrable.

Where there are small trees, they are perhaps only two metres tall although they may be up to 20 years old. However, when a giant tree falls and opens a hole in the canopy these smaller trees race upwards to the life-giving light. Until then they wait.

From *Rainforests* by Stephen Jones

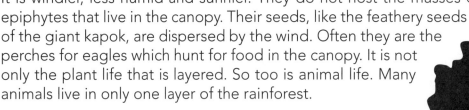

Reading and Comprehension

1. Most life in the rainforest is found
(a) in the canopy.
(b) under the ground.
(c) on the ground.
(d) above the canopy.

2. Energy for the rainforest comes from
(a) the trees.
(b) the animals.
(c) the sun.
(d) the canopy.

3. It is easy to walk through a rainforest with a thick canopy because
(a) there are few trees there.
(b) there is little vegetation.
(c) the trees grow tall.
(d) only big trees fall down.

4. What name is given to the tallest trees?

_____

5. Number the following events (1–4) in regards to when an old tree dies and falls.
(a) Smaller trees grow to take its place.
(b) Sunlight gives plants energy.
(c) A hole opens in the canopy.
(d) Light is allowed in.

Spelling and Vocabulary

Rewrite the misspelt words.

6. The rainforrest is teaming with life.

_____

7. Frogs are a memeber of the family of amfibians.

_____

Circle the word that has the nearest meaning to the underlined word.

8. Rainforests are <u>humid</u>.
(a) hot
(b) wet
(c) hot and wet
(d) dark

9. <u>Reptiles</u> live in the canopy.
(a) birds
(b) snakes and lizards
(c) spiders
(d) insects

Circle the correct word in brackets.

10. This is the (tall, taller, tallest) tree in the forest.

11. The plants are (meters, metres) tall.

12. In the rainforest (its, it's) difficult to see.

Grammar and Punctuation

13. Rewrite these three sentences as one sentence. Don't use *and*.

Giant kapok trees have seeds. The seeds are feathery. They are dispersed by the wind.

_____

_____

_____

_____

14. Punctuate and capitalise this text.

many creatures (spiders insects birds reptiles mammals and amphibians) are to be found in the rainforest canopy our teacher told us

_____

_____

_____

_____

© 1998 Harval Pty Ltd and Pascal Press
Reprinted 1999, 2000, 2001, 2003, 2004, 2006, 2007, 2008 (twice), 2010, 2011 (twice)

Updated in 2013 for the Australian Curriculum

Reprinted 2014, 2015, 2016, 2018, 2019, 2020, 2021, 2022, 2023

ISBN 978 1 86441 277 2

Pascal Press
PO Box 250
Glebe NSW 2037
(02) 9198 1748
www.pascalpress.com.au

Publisher: Vivienne Joannou
Australian Curriculum updates edited by Rosemary Peers and
    answers checked by Peter Little
Typeset by Precision Typesetting (Barbara Nilsson)
    and lj Design (Julianne Billington)
Cover by DiZign Pty Ltd
Printed by Vivar Printing/Green Giant Press

Acknowledgements
The following sources for material are kindly acknowledged:
Additional Fables by Rolf Grunseit
My Diary by Jenny Jarman-Walker
Strange Mysteries by Rachael Collinson
The Tooth Book by Viki Wright
Puppets by Carole Hooper
Tell Me How by Mike Callaghan et al.
Antarctica by John Collerson
Beowulf's Downfall by Brad Turner
Earth First by Jenny Dibley and David Bowden
Hoosta! The Story of Camels in Australia by Keren Lavelle
Kites by Jenny Dibley and David Bowden
Technology for the Environment by Mike Callaghan and Peter Knapp
Spacescape by Karl Kruszelnicki
Saving Wildlife by Edel Wignell
Shaping the News by John Fitzgerald
Rainforests by Stephen Jones
Indonesia by Lisa Hill
Made for Australia by Judith Kendra
What's Cooking? by Kerrie Bingle et al